BF
Publishing

Bruises from Within

Karla Reeves

Bellamy-Fleming Publishing
Berea, Kentucky

BF
Publishing

Bellamy-Fleming Publishing
A Division of Parkway Publications, LLC
Berea, Kentucky

Interior design by Jerlene Rose
Cover design by Wizard Graphics

ISBN: 978-1-7361047-0-5

Printed and manufactured in the United States of America.

*I dedicate this book to all who have had
domestic violence touch their lives,
and to the survivors who have had
the strength and courage
to leave the abuse -- men, women,
teens -- young and old.
Abuse can happen to anyone.*

———————

Acknowledgments

I want to thank my husband Donald, love of my life, just for loving me for me, as I am. He has seen me through my very best and my very worst and has shown me that I am loveable. I will always be so grateful for his friendship and love.

God sent me many angels in human form at times of great need. Among them are: Jim, a dear friend and mentor who helped me understand abuse and how it really affects a person; and my good friends, Ada and Glen. Without their help I would not, could not, have left my abuser. Words can't express the love I have for both of them for just being there for me. My friend S.K. whose friendship came at a time when God knew I needed a friend. Sherry B., Mark L., and Marge. I don't know Marge's last name but, from the first day I met her, she was a great counselor. The counselors at Peace River Women's Shelter, and Miss Grace, Victoria's counselor and tutor.

I want to also thank my church family, Westwood Baptist church, for all your prayers and help. I believe God sends you people in your life to help you and God has sent me many people in my life to help guide me. I will forever be grateful that God has given me so much grace in my life. My life is the shades of grace.

What is grace? It is favor with God. This is my testimony of my life. Without God's love and grace, I wouldn't have made it. God has shaped me into the woman that I have become.

I thank Him most of all.

From the publishers

*A*t first glance we realized that Karla Reeves' manuscript would require heavy editing. Karla has dyslexia, a disorder which is characterized by trouble with reading, despite normal intelligence. The brain simply doesn't "see" or process letters in a normal way. Since it was not possible for her to type or hand write her story, she used a voice activated typing machine. The result was a manuscript with virtually no punctuation or paragraphing and sentences that ran from one into another. Complicating things further, words that sound similar by voice, might be translated to paper incorrectly. It was an editor's nightmare. That having been said, her sory needed to be told.

Taking on this project was about Karla's perserverance and her strength of character. It was about her story, her voice, and how, without a publisher, that story might remain silent. Karla's story reminds us that having a disability makes it more difficult for domestic violence victims to break free. Her story also reminds us of how faith can play a part in healing.

Abuse has not stopped in America and the voices of the victims should rise together as a chorus until this is no longer an issue. We knew we had to help Karla tell her story.

Jerlene Rose and
Janice Odom

Karla Reeves

- ONE -

Putting a Face on Domestic Violence

In writing this book, I wanted to put a face on domestic violence. I am the face of domestic violence. It's my face, but it is potentially the face of any woman. It could be your face.

One day, I looked in the mirror. The hardest thing I had to do was to take a long, hard look at myself and admit that I was an abused woman. Like many women, I had been living in denial. The hardest thing for me to say out loud was, "Karla, you are in an abusive relationship."

You can't imagine how those words stuck in my throat. I felt like a piece of meat was choking me. The knowledge was suffocating. But this was the reality that I was living. A person cannot see what they refuse to see in themselves. That's what denial is -- refusing to see what is right in front of you. In my case it was the abuse. I had to learn to see the ugliness of abuse.

It is my sincere hope that by sharing my journey, and allowing you to walk in my shoes, that you will see the abuse, and the victim, through my eyes. I want you, my readers, to fully understand why so many abused women stay in the cycle of abuse. I know from experience that these women, these victims, are so misunderstood. Perhaps if you feel my pain from my words, then it will help you to avoid the pain that I endured. It may also help you understand the emotional and psychological damage caused by abuse, and why it is so hard to leave. Why so many women don't leave.

All people share the common bond of humanity. My words are your words. My pain is your pain. If you have never been abused, here are my shoes. Put them on for a while. With my words I want to paint a picture to make you feel all the emotions that I felt while being broken down by words. There are many people who have been broken down by toxic love. Toxic love isn't really love at all. It is a cruel imitation.

There are so many facets of abuse, like the surface of water that sparkles in sunlight. The dark side of abuse, that so many don't see, lies below the surface, waiting to pull you down and drown your spirit, until finally the toxic abuse kills you. Sometimes the death is physical. More often, it is the emotional and spiritual self that dies. The path of domestic abuse is scattered with many broken spirits, many broken lives.

Domestic violence has no boundaries. Domestic violence does not discriminate. It can be found in all social levels, economic levels, and all education levels. An abuser, or a victim, can come from a wealthy, educated family or from the poorest. Abuse can take many forms. It can be physical battery with all the bruises and broken bones that are visible on the outside. It can be verbal and emotional, breaking down the spirit and self-confidence. It can be controlling and isolating, shutting the victim off from family and friends who might offer support and help. Abuse can happen to anyone at any time of life. It doesn't matter whether they're rich or poor, young or old. Abuse is like a ripple in a pond that eventually affects the whole pond. I hope that for you, or for someone you care about, healing starts with me today.

I remember saying, "Lord, help me through this mess." I had to humble myself to see my life as it really was. I had to be honest with myself. We build walls to hide the ugliness and pain from the world. We build walls to hide the ugliness and pain from ourselves. As long as I didn't admit that I was abused, then I didn't have to face the abuse. I lived my life with lies to others, and I was lying to myself at the same time. I carried those lies on my face. Fake smiles. Fake answers to questions: "I'm ok." "Everything's fine." "He loves me." Sometimes I couldn't even fake a smile. I finally knew, when I looked in the mirror, that there was pain behind those eyes. Seeing and recognizing that fake smile in the mirror made me realize, I had to make the decision to stop lying to myself and to the world, to face the truth, and to get out. I finally came to realize that, as long as I stayed in denial, the abuse would never end.

Living with abuse isn't living. It is a pain that reaches the depths of the heart and soul. I wasn't marked with bruises on the outside, on my face or with a black eye that people could see. I was marked with bruises on the inside.

And yet, sometimes my inside scars were visible to perceptive individuals, especially those who had walked the same path of abuse. Denial was my blindness. Blindness was my denial. On some level, even I knew that the fake world that I lived in would one day shatter like a mirror. When that day finally came, I had to put my life back together like a puzzle. That was the day I really saw my true reflection for the first time. When I looked deeply into my soul, I saw the brokenness. Things that I had turned a blind eye to were now visible. I had thought denial was protecting me. That was the biggest lie I had told myself, and I had started to believe my own lies.

A truth all victims eventually must face is that living in denial will never make your abuser change. Say this to yourself: "Living in denial will never make my abuser change." Repeat it as many times a day as you need to, to give you strength and courage. You have to want a different life. You have to take a good look in your mirror. Until you acknowledge you are in an abusive relationship, your healing will never start.

Victims often live under the false belief that they can change their abuser. One thing to remember is that nobody can change another person. Your love will not change them or make them different. Have you ever heard yourself say, "My love will change our relationship?" We hear their apologies and want to believe: "This time it will be different." "I'm sorry." "I didn't mean to hit you." "I love you." We want to believe, "This time it will be different." Trust the voice of experience. It won't. Abusers are emboldened by our acceptance, by our forgiveness. And each time, the abuse gets worse.

It is important to realize another truth. The abuse is not just hurting you. It is hurting your children. They are learning a false narrative of what a normal relationship looks like. I suffered the abuse, but the person I hurt the most by living in denial was my little girl. For her sake, I had to see beyond the illusion I had created by denial and lies.

There is pain from the abuse, and there is pain in healing, too. To get out of an abusive relationship, a person has to be willing to take on the pain of healing. My own painful healing process was not nearly as bad as seeing the pain that had been created in my little girl. I had to take the first step. Nobody wants to see their child in pain. If you have suffered from abuse, or are suffering from abuse, let today be your first step. It is the hardest, but it is worth it.

My healing process began with God. If you are dealing with abuse, yours can, too. Step forth and be healed in Jesus's name. "By His stripes I am healed!" Say it! Repeat it often. Jeremiah 29:11. "For I know the plans I have for you," declares the Lord, "plans to prosper you and to not harm you, plans to give you hope and peace, and a future." Stand on that promise with faith and the grace of God.

There are so many reasons why a woman will stay in an abusive relationship, and so many myths. I've heard people say that some women are "turned on" by being hit. That is a myth. No one wants to be hit. An abuser might tell himself, or herself, that the person they're abusing enjoys the abuse, but this is only a way to excuse the behavior. The abuser lies to himself to make himself feel better. And, yes, a woman can be an abuser, too, and it can be even harder for a man to admit that he is a victim of spouse abuse. So, if you are a man in an abusive relationship, this message is for you, too.

We know hitting is not love. Love does not hurt. It is as simple as that. The longer a person stays in an abusive relationship, the more they put their lives and their children's lives at risk. These abusive relationships will not get any better unless the abuser gets help, gets counseling, and takes anger management classes. Unfortunately, that rarely happens. Some abusers suffer from mental conditions like sociopathy. These individuals do not experience emotion and are incapable of change. Because of their lack of emotion, they don't even see a problem. Sociopathy is not denial; it is a total lack of empathy and is even more frightening and dangerous. In these instances, the victim must seek help for themselves.

Abuse can happen at any stage in your life. Abusers choose to abuse. He or she needs to be responsible for their actions. You are not responsible. Don't let them make you believe that the abuse is your fault. Oftentimes the abuser will try to make you believe that it's you that caused him or her to hit you. They will never take accountability for the damage that they do to you.

Sometimes we romanticize our relationships. We convince ourselves that our abuser is the "love of our life." The truth is, we just missed the cues. We weren't paying attention when we heard the stories of how he battered his ex-wives or ex-girlfriends. That should have been our red flag. Or, because we had not yet seen that side of our partner, we couldn't believe that this person, who has been so sweet and attentive to you, could possibly be as bad as the ex-girlfriend or ex-wife says. "They must be lying because they are jealous or vindictive," you think. Even if your partner doesn't have an arrest record of battery, that doesn't mean that they did not abuse their previous partners. It does not mean they won't or are not abusing you, or that somehow, it's your fault that they are hitting you.

If your partner is a batterer and doesn't have an arrest record, this only means that he hasn't been caught, or that his past victims were not strong enough to make those charges and stick to them. Many abuse victims drop charges out of fear of retaliation, or they believe the abuser when they promise "never again." Don't believe it. It will happen again. It always happens again.

If his ex-partner tells you that he has beaten her or him, listen. If they beat their ex-partner, then chances are he will beat you, too. The abuser won't change their behavior until they receive mental health care. Again, I say, please understand that your love for them will not be the miracle to change or transform them. Changing their behavior is totally up to them. The abuser has to first admit that they are abusive. If they don't "own" what they do, then they will never change. Be careful. He or she certainly won't change just because you love them. You loved them before they hit you. It didn't make a difference then, and it won't make a difference now.

There can be all kinds of reasons why a person becomes a batterer. Maybe he saw his father beating his mother. He may equate that with "normal" behavior. Remember this: Your life and your children's lives are worth love – true, genuine, beautiful, caring love. Not a pseudo-love that leaves you miserable and broken.

Here are your test questions to ask yourself to help you determine if you are being abused:
- Are you afraid of your partner or their temper? Seriously, ask yourself that question. Are you?

- Are you relieved when they are asleep or passed out?
- Are you fearful when they are home?
- Are you fearful when they are drinking? Be really honest with yourself.
- Does he call you a "bitch" or a "tramp?"
- Does he call you names in front of your children or friends?
- Does he belittle you, call you "stupid," or make fun of you? This is verbal, emotional, and mental abuse to you and your children who are watching and listening. Your abuser is trying to make you believe you are "less than."

If your abuser tells you stories of how his father beat his mother, pay attention. There is a good chance he will beat you. If you are dating, watch how his parents treat one another. Examining the way your abuser was raised can give you clues. Watch his mother when his father is around. Does she act nervous or cautious? Is she afraid to speak up or voice an opinion? Pay attention to how your partner treats his mother. If he does not treat his mother with affection and respect, how do you think he will treat you?

If you can relate to what I've written and the questions that I ask you to ask yourself, then maybe you have been living in denial. If you can see yourself in these sentences and in these words, you are in an abusive relationship. The way that they treat you in a relationship is the way that they will treat you when you are married. It won't get better; it will only get worse.

Another aspect that an abuser will work on is your relationships with family and friends. The abuser will try to cut you off from all your friends and family. The abuser will create rules for you to live by. You could be told that you can't speak to certain members of your family, certain friends, and members of the opposite sex. Remember, no one owns you. You are no one's possession. It doesn't matter if you are married to them or not, you are no one's property.

When you were young you needed your parents. Your father or mother may have made rules for you that were designed to protect you. The person you are in a relationship with is not your parent. If they have rules they set for you, they are not designed to protect you. They are designed to control you.

- TWO -

The Beginning

When "Roy" and I first met, he put on his best face. I couldn't see who he really was. He spoke so kindly and so softly, and I was so young and naïve. He insisted that we keep our relationship a secret. I know now that the reason he had me keep our relationship a secret was that I was only 16, and he was 27 years old. He was afraid of being arrested for statutory rape. Love is not secretive. If your boyfriend or "significant other," wants your relationship to be a secret, that's a red flag.

Roy was typical of abusers. They put on a big act until they get what they want. After I moved in with him it didn't take long for me to begin to see who he really was. He changed from the kind, sweet person I thought he was. This change was because he didn't have to act anymore. He could relax and be who he really was -- a controlling abuser.

Sometimes Roy would say things to me that were belittling. He would tell people that he had "taken me to raise." Think about that. Is that a loving statement? What he was truly saying was that he took me to train and control. He would always tell me that if I would just "mind" him and do as he said, that everything would be fine. Was I a dog that he was training? No, I wasn't. I was treated like a pet, but I was, I am, a human being.

He would tell me that I "never listened." Unfortunately, at the time, I did listen, and I tried to comply with his nonsensical rules. But as hard as I tried, I could never please him.

At first, the abuse was mostly verbal, pulling my self-esteem down further, and it was designed to instill fear. He tried to make me believe that he knew everything, and I knew nothing. He tried to make me feel worthless and incapable of taking care of myself, especially if I threatened to leave him.

There was so much about Roy that I didn't know and didn't find out for a long time. The lies he fed me were numerous. While we were still just "seeing" each other, he suddenly left for Texas "for work" he said. I didn't know at the time that he was forced to leave the area because he had written a whole bunch of bad checks and there were warrants out for him in Fayette, Clark, Powell, and Montgomery counties and he was about to be arrested. After a few weeks, he drove back from Texas, picked me up and I left with him.

Far away from family and friends, with no resources or money of my own, I was at his mercy and the abuse, of course, got worse. Eventually, I managed to call my dad and told him I wanted to come home. He was still angry because I had run off with Roy. He said, "You've made your bed; now lie in it." I was stuck. I had to make the best of it.

I learned pretty quickly, that if I did what Roy said, things were a little easier, at least when he was sober. But he was demanding and often cruel, both verbally and physically. I learned to "obey," to do what he wanted and the way he wanted. I became the very best housekeeper you will ever see, because he used any excuse to belittle me. The floors had to shine, the dishes washed and put away, beds made, laundry clean. If he spotted dust on a table, it was "What the h--- have you been doing all day?" I cooked, making what he liked and how he wanted it cooked, and if it didn't suit him, he'd toss the plate on the floor, tell me I was stupid and that I couldn't do anything right, and to get down and clean it up. I learned that it was easier to do that than to get into a fight and get slapped, pushed and shoved around, or worse.

20

Another thing I didn't know about Roy was that he was still legally married when he picked me up and took off to Texas with me. I didn't find that out until his wife filed for divorce and child support. It took her and the court quite a while to track him down. Unwittingly, it was I that enabled them to find him. But I'm getting ahead of myself.

We stayed in Texas eight years. One day his brother showed up in their mother's truck. He had taken it without her knowledge, with the intention, on instructions from her husband, to torch it for the insurance. Later, her house burned, and although I can't prove it, I suspect that was an insurance burn, too. Her husband took her on an outing and, lo and behold, the house caught fire and burned to the ground.

Roy's brother wanted to go to Florida. They pulled out a map and spread it out over the table, looked it over, pointed to a town and said, "How about here?" It was Lakeland, Florida. So that is what we did – loaded up the vehicles and headed to Florida. I had no say in the matter, but my feeling was, it got me a little closer to Kentucky. I figured that was a good thing, so I kept my mouth shut, just as I had been trained to do.

We found a place to live; Roy found a job. The abuse continued. One thing did change. Since Roy believed the "statute of limitations" had run out on the cold check warrants, he took me home to Kentucky for a week of "vacation" to visit my family -- my first visit in a long time. That's when I really learned a lot of truths about Roy.

My dad sat me down and said, "I need to tell you some things." Dad had a friend in the police department in Montgomery County, and the friend had told him all about Roy's long "rap sheet" of illegal activity. Apparently, besides writing cold checks, Roy had done some illegal gun-running, drugs, and more. Still, I went back to Florida with him. I was entrenched in the life we'd built together. I didn't know I had options to do otherwise. Roy had kept me isolated, under his rule and control. I had no job skills, no money of my own, could not drive, and I was afraid of what Roy would do if I tried to leave. Adding to that, I had Dyslexia, which made it very difficult to read anything. Letters and words were just a jumble to me. Roy used my lack of reading skills to belittle me, calling me stupid and further damaging my self-image.

As the years passed, Roy drank more, his moods gradually became more unpredictable, and the violent rages more frequent. I didn't know what had caused the change. I was constantly walking on eggshells to not upset Roy and cause an outburst of violence. Now, looking back, I think he was not only drinking more, but using drugs, possibly cocaine.

Roy had always been jealous of me, and suspicious that I was going out on him when he was away at work or gone somewhere with his friends. He would accuse me and no amount of denying it appeased him. In a jealous rage, he would rip off my clothes, stip me down and examine every inch of my naked body for evidence of cheating. Even to looking in my mouth. It was beyond humiliating and frightening. I never had cheated on Roy. I was too afraid to even think of it.

One time, Roy took me to a doctor. Roy had insisted on going in the office for the consultation and was sitting beside me when the doctor told me that I had an STD and gave me a prescription. He said, apparently, I had been with someone. I quickly spoke up and said, "No I haven't been with anybody except my husband. If I caught something, I got it from him." Roy looked down and didn't say a word. He knew he was the one doing the cheating.

Sex was one of the things Roy used against me. If he came home drunk and I didn't want to have sex, he'd accuse me of "givin" it to somebody else, "since you ain't givin' it to me." Many times, whether I was willing or not, he would force himself on me, often in a violent way, taking his anger out on my body. That is spousal rape, but there is little a woman can do about it. It is sometimes hard to prove, and the general attitude is that the husband has conjugal rights to have sex from his wife.

I threatened to leave many times, but he had plenty to say about what would happen to me if I didn't have him to take care of me. He told me that no one would want me because I was fat. After I had my daughter, he told me that no one else would want me because I had a child. He knew how to manipulate me by saying things that made me feel inferior and worthless. Roy used those words to beat me down emotionally and psychologically, to make me submissive so he could control every aspect of my life.

Fear is another method that abusers use as a method of control. If I tried to rebel against his rules, or when his words didn't work, he would tell me that if he couldn't have me, no one else would. Those words were a death threat. There were other veiled threats as well. He would tell me that I was the reason that men "go postal" and blow up buildings.

One time his mother-in-law from his second marriage called him. I couldn't hear her side of the conversation, but I certainly remember what he said to her. He told her, "I will burn your house down and you in it, you bitch." You could tell that he meant every word he said. The person who can make these kinds of comments is very dangerous. Don't mistake comments like this as a joke.

When you decide you've had enough; when you decide to leave the abusive relationship, prepare well. If children are involved, some men don't want to pay child-support. If they feel threatened by you leaving and filing for child-support, this can give them reasons to harm you and maybe even your children. If, on the other hand, they don't want you to take the children with you and there will be a custody battle, be equally careful. Have a support system in place. Have a safe place to go. Get yourself into a good counseling program that can help you learn to break the cycle of abuse.

When you do decide to make the break and leave your abusive relationship, there are things you should and should not do. First, do NOT tell him you are leaving. That can bring things to a violent head and his anger could quickly become deadly. Many women, and children too, have been killed by a spouse who won't let them leave. Sometimes it's jealousy. Sometimes it's selfishness. "If I can't have you no one else can." "You're not taking my kids away from me." "No other man is going to raise my kids." "You're not getting a penny out of me for child support." Either way, for whatever reason, it can turn deadly.

Second, do prepare ahead, secretly and quietly. Find a person you trust and if you don't have someone, then call the ABUSE hotline or a women's shelter and they will advise and help you escape safely. Gather up legal papers that you might need and put them in a safe place where you can grab them and go. Papers you might need are Social Security cards, birth certificates, marriage license, and bank statements that might prove income. All these are helpful in establishing your legal rights. But don't be discouraged from leaving if you don't have them. Leave when you can do so safely, with or without papers.

When you get out of the relationship, do stay out. Don't flaunt a new boyfriend in their face. Don't tempt him. Many will keep the promise and kill the one that they are threatening, and sometimes anyone standing in the way. Make a clean break from the relationship. If they make threats, you need to "run to the nearest exit." You need to call 911.

Soon after leaving an abusive relationship is when you are most vulnerable to getting back into that same abusive relationship, or another one just like it. The tendency is to choose the same type of person again, fall for the same stories. I have learned that the first year that you get out of an abusive relationship is when he will try to pull out all the stops to win you back. If you weren't married, he may propose to you. If you were married, the promises and apologies will flow like honey. If you wanted a child, he will promise to start the family you wanted. You will want to believe the promises and apologies, but don't believe any of it. Harden your heart. Protect yourself from your own weaknesses. Surround yourself with a support system: counseling, family, friends.

It took me twenty years – yes, twenty years – of abuse and fear, to get up the courage to leave my abusive relationship. One month after I left Roy, he proposed to me, trying to win me back. Those first two years after you leave an abusive person are the hardest. Don't go back. Not even if they offer you a wedding ring or promise the baby you wanted to start your family. During this time, sometimes referred to as the "honeymoon," the abuser will do and promise anything to win you back. They will be on their best behavior. It will be like he is in church. There may be lots of gifts and promises. They will say all the right things for a while. They promise that it will be different this time. Don't fall for it. A few weeks after you take them back, the façade will crumble, and then the abuse is usually worse. The attitude is, "How dare you think you can leave me and get away with it!"

Roy was first and foremost an alcoholic. That was a red flag that, at first, I didn't know, then I ignored. I didn't realize what that might mean to our relationship. Not all abusers are alcoholics, but, for the unfortunate victims of abuse, the combination of abuse and alcohol can be deadly. I knew that he needed to be in a hospital or in treatment to stop drinking, and he promised me that he would stop drinking. Those promises were just ploys and tricks to get me back. Unless your abuser gets some type of counseling to show you that he is truly willing to change, he won't change. I will guarantee you one hundred percent that your abuser will get worse. Without counseling the relationship is doomed. And the longer it continues, the greater chance that your life is at risk.

If you stay in the relationship, I urge you to get into counseling, even if he won't. Go to Al-Anon, which is a support group for families and friends of alcoholics. Or go to an AA meeting, which is designed for alcoholics. Hearing the personal stories of alcoholics may be the eye opener that you need. It may provide the reality check that opens your eyes.

The best thing you can do is to develop a support network. If you can find someone who has been through domestic violence and gotten out, that is also very helpful. You can often find support through church. It is often helpful to find a group of church ladies to befriend. Emotional support is important. Find a friend.

For whatever reason, some victims may not have family, or they may be estranged from family. In just a short time, in our relationship, I didn't feel like I had any family to go to. Roy had gradually isolated me from my entire family. If I was "good" I might convince him to let me have a phone. This usually lasted only a short while, then he would say the bill was too high and have the phone cut off and there were no more phone calls to my family. This is another form of control, of mental and emotional abuse.

He would give me rewards. But these were only temporary. He would take them away almost as quickly as they were given. These rewards were things like cable television or Internet access. His control was exercised over everything. He had all the power. He controlled the food I ate, because we only bought things he liked. He controlled who I could see or talk to and for how long. He controlled whether or not I had a car to drive or even a driver's license. I didn't learn to drive until several years after leaving Roy.

Roy would threaten me in so many ways. Sometimes he would just find a reason to pick a fight with me. He seemed to get perverse pleasure out of playing mind games with me. He was training me to not speak my mind. If I voiced an opinion or spoke my mind, I was punished.

"Punished?" you ask. Yes, punished. I learned the hard way to keep my mouth shut. He would put me out of the car and leave me to get home on my own. He wasn't worried about what might happen to me. A man who loves you would never put your life in danger by putting you out of his car on the side of the road in the middle of the night. But that's exactly what he did to me.

That happened one night when we had been invited to the home of one of his friends that he worked with. As the evening got later and he got more and more drunk, he started yelling at me and saying things like he did when we were at home. I was so embarrassed and ashamed. His friends had never seen him in one of his abusive moods and were shocked. I wanted to go home.

Finally, we left, and in the car, he continued the fight, calling me everything, driving fast and wild. I was so scared. When I tried to get him to slow down or let me drive, that just made him crazy mad. He slowed the car, reached across and opened my car door and pushed me out onto the side of the road, yelling, "Bitch, you don't like my driving. You can walk." We were miles out in the country and I really had no idea where we were, or where I was. I lost my shoes when he pushed me out of the car. I don't know how far I walked in the pitch-black dark, just following the road, until finally, after what seemed like hours, someone from the party drove by and saw me, picked me up and took me home. When word got back to his friends what he had done, that ended the friendship. They couldn't believe someone would do that to their wife.

The abuse was like a song in my head that he would play over and over. He would tell me I was nothing. He would remind me that I had no job and no car, that I was strapped down with a baby and that I had nothing. If you hear words like this often enough, the danger is, you start to believe them. I had to empower myself. We should all learn how to drive and get our education and job skills. You never know when you might need those skills.

There were many kinds of punishment Roy used on a daily basis. Sometimes, if we had Internet, I would get on the computer while Roy watched his sports programs on television. When I got off the computer, he would check my search history demanding to know what I was doing and demanding to see all my e-mails and have my passwords. When I asked why he wanted my passwords he would get more enraged and fight with me.

I recall a time when I was typing on the computer and Roy was trying to talk to me. It made him angry that I was on the computer instead of giving him my undivided attention. So, I tried to show him some respect and I closed out the screen. He asked me if I was online talking to somebody. I tried to assure him that I was not. He slammed a $90 flashlight down in front of me and broke it, and told me, "Next time it will be your hands!" This is intimidation, designed to instill fear and obedience, and it was effective. I was scared. And I stayed scared most of the time. Afraid to voice an opinion; afraid not to voice an opinion.

Roy really didn't need a reason to get upset or pick a fight. He was always possessive of me. No matter what I did it would always be wrong. There were times when Roy could intimidate me and instill fear in me just by looking at me. He didn't always have to say threatening words. Sometimes just the glare from him would have me shaking. I could never please him. I was damned if I did, and damned if I didn't.

Roy wanted to control everything about me. I felt like I was on a roller coaster going up and down the hills. I was always tense. The honeymoon phase was the calm, bottom of the roller coaster ride. Then he would start being agitated, or drinking, and the fear and anxiety would build up in me, knowing his temper would explode like a firecracker. It was pure insanity, pure madness. There was no sense to what would set off his anger and rage.

Remember, nobody owns you. No one has the right to control

you. Watch and listen to their words carefully. How they speak to you will tell you something. How they speak to others will tell you even more.

- THREE -

Guilt and Shame

It took me twenty years to leave Roy. When I did finally leave, I felt like my emotions were in a blender. As I said, it is important that you don't get into another relationship soon after getting out of an abusive one. Not for love and not just to have help paying your rent. Depend on yourself. You need to start healing from your abusive relationship. I would implore you to get counseling because the counseling will help you to get back your self-esteem. And getting into counseling will also bring you into contact with resources that can help you find other kinds of support, like housing, employment, continuing education. My years with Roy had shattered my self-esteem and it took years to repair that damage. I will confess to you that I still have self-esteem problems. There are still times when that old feeling of being "less than," or feeling insecure or helpless, will pop up and I have to fight for control over it.

Abuse filled my life with a never-ending feeling of guilt and shame. The shame kept me hiding the secret of abuse. I hid it for 20 years. Shame's partner is guilt. Shame and guilt will keep you in a cell of pain, but confronting that guilt and shame made my pain begin to heal. I am my harshest judge, and you will be, too.

I judge myself for staying in the abuse. How could "the girl next door" end up in a relationship with that type of abuse? I had no sympathy for myself. I was consumed with shame and guilt. I felt that I would be judged by people. Then I deflected my feelings of shame and guilt from myself and placed it on the ones that seemed to be judging me.

Why didn't I validate my abuse and speak out about it? I came from a culture that taught me in childhood that you do not speak of a husband hitting his wife. If abuse happened in your family, it was just your shame to bear. This corner of dark silence was a woman's lot in life. We have been taught for generations that a woman must bear the shame and abuse without daring to speak about it. That wall of silence surrounded things that we did not discuss. Abuse in the family was accepted and thus enabled to keep on going. I should have spoken out and validated myself when no one else would. I needed to give power back to myself. Most of all I needed to find my voice. But how was I to get my voice back when years of acceptance was part of my culture?

Somehow, with God's help, I found the courage to share my story of abuse. As of today, I am taking off that dirty coat of silent shame, and pain, and guilt. With God's grace and strength, I will make it. I want to change the way women are taught. Women are not to blame for what the abuser does. And for me that cloak of shame and silence is just too tight for me to wear, ever again.

Speaking up and speaking out about abuse gives you power. Speaking up and speaking out will also help strengthen others. There are people in abusive relationships that need our helping hand of compassion and love. I am reaching out by sharing my life story. I know I will be judged by people for writing about my family's "dirty little secrets." Some people may be uncomfortable that I've shared the secrets behind my abuse. But I know that, no matter what, I am walking in the grace and favor of God.

I'm not writing about the things that happened in my life to ever hurt or shame anyone. In my case, many lessons were taught to me, and there were some unhealthy ideas about abuse that I embraced. I only knew the lessons that I was taught by my mother and my grandmother. They taught me to keep it all inside, the way that they had been taught.

I can now tell you that abuse can never heal if it isn't brought to the surface. We must do better than this. The mindset of previous generations must stop! We can teach from the heart of compassion and not pain. These old lessons only birth more pain and perpetuate cycles of abuse.

Like most young girls, I grew up hearing fairytales. These fairytales were about a man on a white horse who would save me and take me away from all the unpleasantness of life. All the Cinderella storybook endings were "happy ever after." In the real world, things are very different. I didn't understand that the Sleeping Beauty stories were only fairy tales. There was always a happy ending in the story. Mom never told me that I needed to be the hero of my fairytale, and that the abuse would never end unless I ended it. She never told me that there was something better than a life full of lies and denial. That there was no magic spell to make it all end. That I could turn to God for his help. But, finally, I did. She was never able to be the hero of her own story. How could she help me be the hero of mine?

I learned that there is nothing to be gained by keeping the code of silence. Death may be the only prize. No one has a right to hit you. You belong to God. Look carefully at your life. Where do those seeds of abuse come from? Where does this behavior come from?

I am just a person that has learned about abuse from my own experience and from the generations of women and men in my life. This is only my opinion of where abuse comes from.

I believe a baby is born with a clean chalkboard, a clean slate. The child is taught many things. I believe what happens to a child in the early years of their lives form the basis for who the child becomes. Maybe the child will be timid. Or maybe the child will be aggressive. I believe those early years form the personality of who the child becomes in life. A child is not born with fear, hate or even love. All of those things are taught.

Those early, formative years were the timeframe of when my own abuse started. I lived in a household that would be called dys-functional. Ours was certainly not an "Ozzie and Harriet" happy family. My mother had mental health issues and her moods and personality were unpredictable, at best. It was that dysfunctional background that made me more vulnerable to Roy.

I was young, barely 16 when Roy came into my life. He was hand-some and he paid attention to me. I was attracted to him. I had a low self-image and he used this to entice me. He would flatter me and tell me how pretty I was and that I would be pretty in new clothes. He would buy me clothes, things he would like me to wear. He wasn't my dad. I wasn't a child being told what kind of clothes to wear. I had sense enough to know how to dress. He wasn't telling me how to dress; he wasn't saying that I dressed like a tramp, or that I dressed like a child. He was telling me how to dress so that he could control what I wore. Does any of this sound like your life? If it does, I invite you to take a closer look.

All those 20 years that I was with Roy, I wasn't happily married. I moved in with him, thinking that "someday soon" we would get married and live the "happily ever after" fairy tale. That didn't happen. Our relationship was built on lies. Eventually, deep in-side, I knew that answers would come only from God. That belief came from my childhood years when I learned about God by go-ing to the Assembly of God church where my paternal grandfather was pastor. And when Roy and I moved to Florida, I regularly went to the church where our landlady attended in Winterhaven. Our landlady, Ada, became a friend and my support.

I had been with Roy for about 12 years when I got pregnant. I was

28 years old when our daughter was born. I was thrilled. It was one of the things I had dreamed of – having a baby to love and nurture and watch grow up. I don't know why, but I thought Roy would be pleased and happy about it, too. Of course, I was wrong.

When the time came for my delivery, I knew I was going to have a Cesarian, and would not be able to do much physical activity. The week before I was to go to the hospital, I cleaned the house from top to bottom and got all the laundry done so I would not have to do much when I came home. But when I got out of the hospital and came back home, the house was a wreck. It seemed like Roy had deliberately made messes throughout the house. He yelled for me to get my ass out of bed and clean up the house and cook his meals. And I did. I was afraid not to.

When I was in the hospital, one of the nurses who was so kind to me, said, "Honey, you need to get rid of that asshole of a husband. While you were up here having a C-section, he was out there flirting with every nurse on the floor." I didn't say anything. I thought, "When we get home with our beautiful little daughter, Roy will change." Unfortunately, things just got worse. Now there was a child who needed my attention. Roy resented that.

I remember when my daughter was eight months old. She was cutting teeth and had been crying off and on most of the day. We were living in a big house. Roy was in a bad mood and he yelled for me to "shut that kid up." I told him she was teething and that I had given her something for her teeth. She kept crying and before I knew what he was doing, he jumped up and went stomping up the stairs. I ran behind him and pushed my way past him into her room.

He yelled at her. He shouted, "Shut the hell up before I shut you up!"

I jumped in front of him and grabbed my baby. I cradled her to stop him from hitting her. He grabbed the leg of the baby bed and slammed the bed down to the floor. It scared my daughter and me. I yelled at him, "Please don't. You are not going to hit my baby. Stop this!"

He grabbed me by the arm and pushed me hard. I fell against the wall with my daughter in my arms. He drew his hand back as if he would slap me. I yelled, "Stop it, stop it. You are not hitting me."

He went back downstairs cussing and yelling. I went to the master bedroom and locked the door. There was a bathroom off the bedroom, and I went in there and locked that door for further protection. Roy had lost his temper and scared the baby. I gave her a warm bath and rocked her to sleep.

I put her in her bed and closed the door. Then I went back downstairs to see where Roy was and if he was still mad. Thankfully, he was passed out on the couch. About an hour later there was some banging at the door. Roy answered the door. It was two police officers. One of them was a lady police officer and the other a policeman.

"We are here to check on Karla," he said. He also said my last name. Not many people in the neighborhood knew my last name, only the neighbors who lived on either side of our house. When the police had knocked at the door, I had gone into the downstairs bathroom. I really don't know why I cowered in the bathroom.

The police wanted to see me. They said they wouldn't leave until they saw me. I made an excuse. I told them I was only wearing a nightgown. The lady police officer said, "Karla, it's okay. I just want to see if you and your daughter are okay."

I came out of the bathroom. The male police officer was talking to Roy. The lady officer and I went upstairs. I told her my daughter was asleep. I turned on the light and she looked around. She told me the neighbors had heard us fighting and had heard a thud like someone had fallen.

The police asked if we were fighting. The truth was that his actions had been abusive by any measure, but that's not what I told the police. He had no right to put his hands on me, or my daughter. If I had told the truth he would've gone to jail that night for battery. But Roy had taught me that what he did wasn't hitting. He had not used his fist. According to Roy, slapping and pushing was not hitting. So, I told them "No, Roy had not hit me." Roy had taught me well. He had changed the way I saw many things.

Even though, deep down, I knew I should have said, "yes," I couldn't tell her the truth. I thought that Roy would be taken off to jail. That would mean that we would be homeless. The officer wanted me to take off my daughter's clothes to ensure that she wasn't bruised. She also wanted me to undress to see if I had any bruises. She assured me that I could tell her the truth. But I was too scared. I couldn't tell her what really happened. Roy had taught me to lie for him. As I lied, I felt like a coward, and I was ashamed.

When they finally left, I went to the upstairs bathroom and cried. I knew I was wrong to not stand up for me and my daughter. Every time something bad happened, Roy would tell me what I saw and experienced. He was grooming me to always defend what he did, even when he was abusive.

Roy would tell me, "I only slapped you. I didn't hit you with my fist." He would go on to say that hitting someone was when you used your fist. That was how he would manipulate me. Many abusers groom you by playing down what they do. It's brainwashing. They want to make you believe they are innocent. Even after they beat you and break your arm or black your eyes. They want you to tell someone that you fell off the porch or ran into a door.

Let me ask you, why should you have to lie when he slaps you or pushes you down the steps? The abuser knows what he or she is doing is wrong. They know they could go to jail. This is why they tell you their version of what happened and want you to believe it. They are protecting themselves, not you.

While I was with Roy, the life lessons I was teaching my daughter were just like my mother had taught me. I was teaching my daughter to stay in abuse; to be silent. When I finally admitted to myself that I was in an abusive relationship that was hurting not only me, but my daughter, I knew I had to do better than this for myself. And most of all, for my daughter. My life's lessons would start with me teaching my daughter. I had to give her a good life example. I had to end my life's deception of lies. The first step was getting rid of the guilt and shame.

The hardest thing I had to learn was learning how to forgive myself. I had to learn to find compassion and empathy for myself. It was easier to forgive anyone else but myself. God had to teach me to forgive myself. I had to forgive myself for what I did to me and my daughter.

You can start today to heal. I have taught myself to forgive myself of toxic shame and a life filled with mistakes. I was like a monarch butterfly. I was in a cocoon, hiding, living my life in abuse. Now I was in the pupa stage of my life. I had to get out. I knew, somehow, I would emerge a new creature through Christ. I knew it would not be easy.

When I moved in with Roy, I weighed 110 pounds. I wasn't fat at all, but Roy would tell me I was fat. Roy's shaming words every day cut me to the quick. The words burned inside my soul. They accomplished breaking my spirit and soul. Roy shamed me into fear and guilt. When you have a relationship built only on shame and guilt and fear, and not love, but something that is full of control and abuse, you need a higher power to help you break away.

When an abuser chooses to hit, he chooses to instill fear. We weren't born with fear. You should never have to fear your mate. We, as babies, weren't born with fear. We've learned to fear. It's not God's will for us to fear. I am learning to overcome the shame that follows me. How could this have happened to me? Not many people knew the hell I was going through, because I hid it so deep. I felt so alone and that no one would help me get away from him. I felt so trapped.

Another hard lesson for me to learn was that I could not make men love me. Young girls, you cannot make boys love you. With Roy, I was living in the world I made up in my mind, but it was a world of fake happiness. It was a life lived inside my head. It had no basis in reality. I wanted Roy to love me so badly that all I could see was what I wanted to see. I couldn't see that his was fake love. I wanted so badly to have a man love me. I wanted to be what he wanted me to be. I wanted to dress like he wanted me to dress in order to gain his love and approval. But I never had his love and approval. I would never get that from him. What I got was being controlled.

A good indication that someone doesn't love you is that they want you to change. People who genuinely love you, they love you for being you. You can be who you are around the people who love you. You don't have to change and conform to be loved. When you try to change just to please someone else, you can lose your own identity. I changed the color of my hair trying to make him love me. These cosmetic changes never made him happy. Deep down, I was always in hell. I didn't even know who I was. Eventually, I had to learn how to be me.

Roy chose my clothes. An example: He'd come in with a "gift" and say, "I got a race jacket for you." This didn't really make me happy. I would've rather had something else, but if I didn't act pleased, he would yell at me. He thought if he liked it, I should, too. I tried to explain to him that I wasn't him. I didn't care for race jackets. Then he would try to make me feel like something was wrong with me for not liking the race jacket. He would say things like, "I just can't please the bitch."

Karla, the real Karla, was lost even to me. I didn't know how to be me. I didn't know what love was supposed to look like. I settled for pretend love. I don't think he knew either, what real love was or how to love.

- FOUR -

Why Do We Stay?

Why did I accept this treatment? Why does anyone? Why do you? It took me a long time to peel back the layers of why I had accepted this mistreatment. I had to dig deep down into my soul to find all the toxic roots of why I allowed the abuse to happen. I think part of the reason was that my early childhood had taught me to stay in abusive situations. Think of your own children and what watching you being abused is doing to them.

I am ashamed to say that it took me 20 years to finally get away from Roy. I tried to leave several times. Each time I tried to leave, we went through that "honeymoon" phase where he would be contrite, apologetic, and make promises to change. He would promise to give up drinking. He would "do whatever would make me happy." He said everything that I wanted to hear. And he would keep those promises for a few weeks, then the tension would start to build, and his behavior would go right back into the same pattern as before. Confronting him was never the answer. He was like a child holding his breath waiting to explode, like when you shake a soft drink. He was always ready to explode. It kept me tense and watchful and stressed.

Karla Reeves

- FIVE -

God Sent Two People to Rescue Me

November 19, 2001. Parts of that day are still hazy. I still only remember bits and pieces. For the longest time I had prayed to God to send someone into my life to help me get out of the abusive relationship that I was in. And He did. He sent two people.

The first was a lady who lived near me. Ada was a great Christian lady. She became like a mother to me. I remember that even on that first day when we met, she told me she would show me what a true friend was. I still call her "Mom" and friend. I won't name her. She knows who she is. This lady took my hand and she told me she knew that I was in a bad relationship. I asked her how she knew. She told me that she knew the first time I came to her house and knocked on her front door. She had told me to come in and I had said, in a timid voice, "I'm sorry to bother you, but...." Apparently, there was something in the way I had said it. In any case, she told me that the timid, apologetic way of starting a sentence is the way a person in an abusive relationship starts a sentence. Do you speak like that? Do you ever find yourself saying, "I'm sorry" for no reason? Think about that.

It is true. That is how I spoke then, and sometimes even now. After she pointed it out to me, I started asking myself, "Why do I apologize every time I open my mouth?" Have you ever asked yourself that question? I had to ask that question and dig down deep into my soul to find answers. All I had done was to knock at her door. I hadn't done anything wrong. I was apologizing for speaking. I had learned to apologize for everything I did. That is one of the results of abuse. I was always saying I was sorry, even if I wasn't in the wrong. Roy kept me in a defensive stance. I was always ready to defend, or apologize, for anything I did.

At the time, I would squirm when my new friend would press me about loving Roy. She would ask me questions about how happy I was or wasn't. I didn't like anyone pressing me or asking me about my life. I didn't want anybody questioning the relationship. Roy had trained me to be defensive. He certainly didn't want anybody prying into our lives. I had learned this defensive behavior from him. Mostly, he had kept me isolated from people. Keeping me away from family and friends kept our secrets safe from penetrating eyes. He brainwashed me into living this way. He convinced me that I didn't need family or friends. All I needed was him.

Roy twisted everything that should have been healthy friendships for me. Roy could have all the men and women friends he wanted. It was only me that wasn't allowed to have friends, even women friends, and certainly not men friends. He didn't want anyone talking to me. He was afraid that I would tell them how abusive he was. Having friends should not be a threat to the person you're in a relationship with. It was a stressful way to live.

Roy was very possessive and accused me of cheating all the time. No matter what I did, Roy made me feel wrong. I want the two friends who helped me to know how thankful I am every day for the freedom they helped me to gain by leaving Roy. The love and compassion they showed to me and my daughter helped me in so many ways.

- SIX -

The Leaving

There was an accumulation of events over a period of about six years that made me decide to finally leave Roy. The abuse had continued to escalate, and the most important thing was, I had found a friend in Ada, our landlord, who lived next door to us. She could hear the fights; she could see me; she was a witness. I couldn't hide the truth from her. She feared for me and my child. We lived next door to her from about 1996 until 2001.

During that time, Roy continued his abuse and unreasonable jealousy. One day I was helping Ada with some work at her house and Roy apparently thought there was a man there. He came running and jumped over her fence and stormed into her house, screaming at me, wanting to know what I was doing, and who I was with.

When Victoria was three years old, Roy came home drunk and high on something. He demanded sex and I refused because he was drunk and acting wild. He flew into a rage. He ripped my clothes off and literally threw me on the bed and proceeded to have sex with me as I tried to fight him off. He was really, really rough. It felt like he was trying to tear me apart inside.

Finally, he got off me and I was hurting and angry, too. I was in a blind rage at what he had just done. I reached beside the bed for a small iron frying pan that I'd put there in case I ever needed it for defense. As he walked down the hall to the bathroom, I walked up behind him and came down on his head with that frying pan with all the strength I had. He fell to the floor and I hit him again and again. I don't know how many times.

Victoria came out of her bedroom where she had been asleep. She looked at her daddy and said, "Daddy inebriated?" I know it sounds funny coming from a three-year-old, but I'd always encouraged her to use big words and not baby talk. I said, "Yes, Sweetie. Daddy's inebriated. Go back to bed. He'll be fine." And she did. She was accustomed to seeing her daddy drunk and passed out in the floor.

Roy was bleeding. I called the police. When they came, they were trying to figure out how I had managed to hit Roy on the head, when he was so much taller than I was. I don't know either. They had me demonstrate. They examined me and noted the choke marks on my neck, bruises on my body and visible signs of the assault. There was no question it was a case of "justified" if not "self-defense," since I'd hit him after the fact.

They took Roy to the hospital and he had to have twenty-seven stitches or staples in his head. He was gone three days. I never knew whether he was in the hospital all that time, or in jail. I didn't care. By this time, he had killed any feelings I'd ever had for him. He finally came back home and never said a word about what had happened. I don't know if he didn't know what I'd done or didn't remember what happened. I never asked him about his stitches, and he didn't offer an explanation.

You'd think that would be enough to make me leave immediately. I didn't leave. But things did change between us. I changed. Yes, he was still an abusive alcoholic. But I found ways to pay him back for his abusive behavior. I became braver, but not brave enough to leave. I put Exlax in his brownies. He selfishly finished the whole pan and suffered the consequences. He had no idea it was the brownies. He never even considered that I would have the courage to do something like that to him. Victoria had asked for a brownie. I said, "No honey, those are for Daddy." I had made a different, small batch for us.

Another time, I put three drops of Ipecac in his beer. He started foaming at the mouth and threw up. He thought he'd gotten hold of a bad beer. I used his toothbrush to clean the commode. Payback can be hell. This silent battle went on for five more years after that terrible assault.

Ada was my support and my encourager. On her advice, I started bringing a few things to her house to hide in her storage building – things I might need if, or when, I made my escape.

There was a satchel that Roy kept by his chair in the living room that he said I was not to touch, ever. But when I finally decided to leave, while he was gone, I looked in it to see what it was that he guarded with his threats of near death. It was all the papers I would need – bank statements, his check stubs, bills, invoices, social security cards, my daughter's birth certificate – all our important papers. I grabbed them and Victoria and ran to Ada's. By this time, Victoria was eight years old.

We got to Ada's house and I was so filled with fear. I was overwhelmed with sheer panic. What if he came back too soon and saw that the papers were gone? What if he caught us before I could leave? What was I doing, tearing apart my daughter's family? She might never get to see her daddy again. What was I doing? I couldn't get my breath. I couldn't talk. I started crying uncontrollably. I was gasping for air. I collapsed to the floor. Ada called 911 and an ambulance came and rushed me to the hospital.

November 19, 2001, will always be my day of Thanksgiving. Saying "thank you" doesn't seem like it is enough. Surely it is inadequate. How do you tell someone "thank you" for saving the lives of you and your child?

That is the day that I woke up in the hospital. I had had a mild heart attack. It scared me nearly to death. God was giving me a wake-up call. I've since learned that stress can be a killer. And being in an abusive relationship is a stressful way to live. It's another way that an abusive relationship can be a killer.

When I woke up in the hospital, they had me hooked up to machines. I was lying in the bed listening to the sound of my heart beating on the monitor. I was making my peace with God, if He should take me that night. I asked God to let me live so I could raise my daughter. I told God how much I loved my daughter and how much I wanted to live. I drifted off for a while into a peaceful sleep.

- SEVEN -

The Doctor Who Saved My Life

About two o'clock the next morning, my cardiologist walked into the room. He asked if he could talk to me. He was an older man. He asked me what brought me to the hospital. He was curious about the circumstances of my life. I looked down as I spoke. I could not look my doctor in the eyes. It wasn't that I was being dishonest with him. My self-esteem was so low I was scared to look anyone in the eyes.

I couldn't get out all the words to say that I was leaving a relationship that was not good, an abusive relationship, and it was stressful. But he understood. He knew.

He said he wanted to take me for a walk in the hospital and asked me if that was okay. I told him sure, it was okay. I didn't know it at the time, but this night would change my life for the rest of my life. Maybe some people would be critical of what the doctor did, but I am grateful for his courage.

I put on my robe and slippers. We went to the elevator. He told me that what he was doing would be frowned upon by some people. I didn't really fully understand what he was saying, but I said, "Okay." I don't remember the thought even occurring to me to say, "No, I don't want to go." Roy had trained me to be obedient.

While we were in the elevator, the doctor told me that he had seen many young women just like me. "We are going to the morgue," he said. I didn't really know why, but I was willing to see what he wanted to show me. As we walked out of the elevator, he told me that he wanted to show me a young girl about my age.

When we walked into the morgue it was just like on TV. It was a sterile environment with doors all over the wall for the bodies. The feeling was just about as creepy as you could imagine. The room was very cold. It was like being in one of those scary movies, but this was all real. Looking all around and hearing the sounds of our footsteps and voices echoing in the room made me feel even more uneasy. He looked for a certain body and pulled it out. It scared me to death. I had never seen a body lying on a slab in a morgue except on TV. I had so many feelings all at once. I was afraid and felt sick. The room started to spin, and I didn't want to lose it and faint, so I took a deep breath. I breathed in and out slowly. I tried to keep a grip; I was so afraid.

As we stood there, he told me the young lady's story. He said "Karla, look at her." That was hard for me to do. I looked at the floor.

He raised his voice and said again, "Look at this young woman, Karla." I could hear an edge of anger in his voice. It triggered my fear and panic.

"She's a mother just like you," he said. "She has three young children. She was beaten to death by her husband. Look, Karla, this is you in a few years."

I felt like a coward. The sheet was pulled up on her body all the way to her neck.

"Just look, Karla. She left her husband and went back to him six months later." The doctor carefully pulled the sheet back. He told me to look at her. He said to really look at her. Could I see myself lying there as she was lying there, beaten to death?

He pulled the sheet off of her and I could see that she was bruised all over. He turned her body over. She had black and blue bruises on her skin and a pale gray, bluish tint. Her lips were bruised all over. Her husband had kicked her in the butt, and you could see the boot print. There was the shape of an iron burnt into her left shoulder. The burn was fresh and deep. How could some animal burn her like she was cattle to be branded? Tears started rolling down my cheeks. How could someone do this to another human being? The doctor said that she was raped postmortem. I just couldn't understand how anyone could do all that he had done to her. There were cigarette burns all over her body. The doctor showed me her ribs where they had been broken. He showed me her nose that had also been broken. He also showed me scars where her husband had stabbed her.

I started to cry hard. The doctor sternly said to me, "Don't you dare cry. This is you."

I asked him, "Why can't I cry?" I held my breath and tried not to cry. I bit my lip. It was overwhelming. I was looking at the brutal truth of how my life could end.

The doctor asked me, "Is your love for this man worth dying for? His love leaves you battered and bruised. Is his love worth leaving your children motherless? Do you have so little value? If you say you're willing to die for his love, then you're a bad mother who doesn't love her daughter."

He asked me to think about this woman's body that was hit, slapped, burned, kicked, and raped. He wanted me to immerse myself in her pain. She had been forced to experience broken bones and busted lips.

I bit my lips harder trying to hold back the tears. I actually tried to hold my breath and not even breathe, but in my mind, I was seeing. I was feeling her pain and torment. For a moment I blinked my eyes and imagined her life as mine. Looking at her, it was like my eyes were taking snapshots from a camera. I viewed her life in my eyes and in my mind. I felt the things that she must've felt as she was on the floor dying. I imagined the warm blood dripping from her face as if it was my blood. I felt the pain of being kicked. There was the knowledge that the pain would only stop when my heart stopped beating. I can imagine feeling her helplessness. What must her last thoughts have been? Was she praying that someone would burst down the door and save her children? Was she afraid that her children would be next? Did she imagine what he would do to them if she wasn't there to protect them?

I heard the doctor's voice. "Imagine her pain as your pain, Karla, of getting kicked with boots on. Feel the pain of loving this man! Feel the pain of him burning her skin. Feel him forcing sex on you while you lay on the floor bleeding and dying, then him spitting on her after he finished violating her. Shaking her like she was a ragdoll and seeing that she wouldn't respond, he dropped her back down to the floor to die. How would you feel seeing him rape your daughter? This is not love. Love does not to this."

"Is this really the kind of love you deserve? If you believe this is real love, then you're wrong. Karla, do you feel her pain? You will certainly feel her pain if you go back to this man. Think about the pain that your daughter must go through when she sees him and hears him abuse you. Your daughter deserves to have her mother in her life. Can you imagine what it would be like if she didn't? She will cry and ask God, 'Why?' She needs a mother to tuck her in at night." I was crying so hard that I was gasping for air as I bit my lips.

"Now look, Karla. That's you, lying there all broken and bruised. Karla, look at your daughter and see her as you tell your little eight-year-old, through lips dripping blood, that this is love? Can you honestly say to her 'Victoria, your daddy loves me'?"

"Can you see your daughter see her, as she sees you? This is what you teach her when you stay with him. You send her a false message that this is love. We teach our children by example. The example that you give her by staying with this man is that love equals blood and broken bones. Someday her father may treat her this way. If it's not her father, perhaps it will be her husband. Children are affected by abuse. When they see you stay, they learn that staying and accepting the abuse is okay. And if you think that she doesn't see it or hear it, then you are lying to yourself. I hope you are beginning to see. That's not love, Karla."

I looked at the poor broken body of the young woman again. I stepped close, even though I was still afraid. I cried, thinking about what she had gone through. When I looked at her wrist, I saw cuttings where she had tried to harm herself. I thought about the many fights that I had had with Roy. I thought about how many times I had wanted to end my own life. But those suicidal thoughts were selfish. How could I think about ending my pain and leaving my daughter to face Roy?

I don't know how long we were in the morgue. The woman was such a frail, thin woman, very small. She probably weighed no more than 120 pounds.

The doctor said to me, "Karla, I showed you this because I wanted to make an impression on you. If you go back to your child's father, this will be you. Take a hard look. Is this what your daughter deserves? Look at your life through your daughter's eyes. She deserves a mother. Can you imagine what your funeral would be like for her? Your daughter is only eight years old. Can you imagine her looking at your body in the coffin? And through her tears she is seeing the bruises all over your body. What will your daughter see?"

"This kind of trauma has an enormous effect on a child, when she sees her beautiful, young mother killed by her father. Do you love her father so much that you will let him kill you? If you stay, this will be you. How do you feel now about loving this man and going back to him? Can you still say that your love for him is worth dying? This is not God's plan for your life, Karla. In God's eyes, you have so much worth. He loves you. God really does love you. God doesn't make the same mistakes that we do. God wants you to wake up and live for your daughter."

"When you stay with him and let him beat you to death, you are teaching your daughter that it's okay to be hit. Think about what you will teach your daughter. What you teach your daughter will last a lifetime, so teach her well. Be careful what you teach her by staying with an abusive man." Then the doctor asked me, "How much do you love your daughter?"

"All there is in this world," I said.

Then he said, "Well then, love your daughter enough to live and leave the father. He will kill you. We don't live our lives asleep. Wake up and see what's going on in your life. See what you're teaching your child. We don't drive our cars asleep. We are awake while driving. Stay awake. Do not accept abuse."

After a time, he told me we were going back to the room. We got back into the elevator and the doctor was speaking to me still. He said, "You destroy your daughter's mind by staying in abuse. Every day you tell your daughter that it's okay to be beaten by the man you love. You may tell your daughter that it's wrong for men to hit you, but by your actions you show her it's okay to be hit. Your actions don't match the life lessons you teach her when you live a lie. When your actions don't match your words, you are living a lie."

I just couldn't get the woman's face and body out of my mind. The bruises and scars all over her kept flashing through my mind.

Then, I would see myself in the coffin. I was seeing my little girl crying for me.

The doctor told me he has seen so many young women go back to the abuser and wind up in the morgue. He told me he wanted to change the way I saw my relationship. He wanted to see me live a different reality. He told me it would be hard, but I could find a support system. He advised me to get into counseling.

On the ride back up to my room, I just saw myself, dead. But the image of my little girl crying for me was one that I couldn't get out of my mind. I thanked the doctor for his help. He hugged me and he said that he had wanted to shock me into living. He told me they would release me in a few days, but he didn't want to see me back in the hospital and especially not in the morgue. He told me I was young and that I if didn't want to live for myself, I should want to live for my daughter. The last thing he told me was that I was going to live, but that I had to make changes in my life. He reminded me that love doesn't hurt or hit you or put you down. Love doesn't hurt.

The doctor left and I laid in bed thanking God that night. I just kept praying for myself and asking God for the strength and help to start my life over again. I wanted to begin living for my daughter.

I don't know what time it was when I finally fell asleep, praying, and I slept the best that I had slept for the first time in years. I'm sure you've heard the old saying that I slept like a baby. Well, I did just that.

*****

I was lying in bed thinking of all the brainwashing Roy had done to me. There were so many things that I was seeing through new eyes that I had refused to see until then. If Roy slapped me and I said, "Don't hit me." Roy would say things like, "I didn't hit you. If I had hit you, I would have punched you in the face. That is getting hit."

- EIGHT -

First Steps to a New Life

I didn't see that doctor again, yet everything that he had said to me kept playing in my head that night and into the next morning. Even so, I fell into a deep, peaceful sleep.

The police had also come to my room and talked with me. The morning after my visit with the doctor, I knew that I had to make a change and take the first steps into my new life. They ran some more tests on my heart and other tests to see if there would be any problems.

The next day my daughter came to see me. I just burst into tears of joy when I saw my little girl. I love her so much. I call her my "ladybug." She sat on my bed and we talked. I told her I couldn't go back to her dad. We had to live apart from him. I was so sorry things had to be that way.

Then, while my daughter was watching TV, she asked me, "Well, are you going back?"

"No," I told her. Then she asked why, "What has changed?"
I told her that I didn't want to talk about it. I also told her that I would never go back to him. She kept trying to drag it out of me. She wanted to understand what had changed. I couldn't tell her what happened, the gruesome thing I had seen in the morgue. I couldn't explain what the doctor had showed me. But I knew that it had changed my life.

I wish that there were more doctors who would scare more women that are battered. It made me change the way I saw my relationship with Roy. Anyway, why would I want to go back to Roy? He had killed off any love that I had had for him.

Even my best friend said she thought I seemed different. "Well, Karla, your game plan sounds good. I just hope you stick with it," my friend said.

"Let me tell you, life is not a game. You don't get any rewinds or do-overs," I said. "I'm done."

"I hope so," she said, as she rolled her eyes.

*****

The police drove me and my daughter to a women's shelter when I was released from the hospital. I never realized how hard my journey would be. I did know that my daughter's life was worth it. I finally felt like my life was worth it, too, and that I had to make myself live for her. I really didn't know where to begin, so I asked God to guide me in every step. I was 36 years old. My whole life had been taken away from me and I had to start over. I didn't know how much I would change. At times it was not easy.

Roy was the only man that I had ever loved. He was like an addiction. I had been dependent on him for everything. Part of that was because he had made me dependent on him by restricting me. He would not let me learn to drive, have friends, or go to school to get my GED. Now, I had to find my own strength, with God's help and guidance.

There were times when I felt like I was falling apart. My mother had not taught me how to do things for myself, how to go about getting my own place. I was only sixteen when I left home and moved in with Roy. I didn't have any job skills. Where I came from, women depended on their husbands for everything. I didn't know how to do anything. For the first time in my life I had to take full responsibility.

I had to do better for my daughter. I owed it to her to get my education. I also owed it to myself. I was worthy of doing better, and I had to keep telling myself that. Now that I knew what abuse was, I had to change my life. I had to break away from the idea that I needed a man to survive. I had to learn not to depend on someone else.

Please understand I am not bashing men, nor am I bashing healthy relationships in which one person works outside the home and another stays home and takes care of the family. Dependency is different; it is a relationship in which the boundaries are unhealthy. It is an excessive emotional or psychological dependency on a partner. This is the type of relationship that I had been living in. Roy had made me believe I was helpless, unable to do anything on my own.

I asked God for his help. The main thing God was teaching me was to lean on Him. It was so hard for me. I wanted to fix things myself, or try to. I always wound up begging God for his help. Sometimes pride stops you from asking for what you need. This was me. I had pride. I couldn't ask for help. God showed me I had to ask for my needs, not only from Him, but from other people. Even though it was difficult at first, I learned to ask for help and to lean on God.

People at the shelter helped me get back into school and helped me find a job. There were so many things I still didn't know how to do. There were so many brand-new things that I had never had to do on my own. I didn't know how to ride the city bus. That probably seems silly to someone who grew up in a city and rode the bus all the time. For me, it was frightening. What if I got off at the wrong place, or took the wrong bus?

I went to the office for Social Services -- what we had always called the "Welfare office." It seemed like I was just another number. I really didn't feel like I was treated like a human being. They told me about all the hoops I would need to jump through to get assistance. It was overwhelming.

The Welfare office told me I had to file for child-support against Roy. They also wanted me to go back to school and get my education. I had to go to school for 20 hours each week, and I had to get a job.

I was so overwhelmed with stress, but I was determined to do this for my daughter, no matter what it took. I enrolled that day for school. I would go to school from 8:00 AM to 12:00 PM, then at 6:00 PM I would go to work. Twice a week I would go to counseling. Fitting everything into my schedule was hard, but I was going to make it. While I was trying to do this juggling act, I did a lot of praying. I found a part-time job cleaning hotel rooms. I didn't have any other work skills. I had been completely dependent on Roy for everything.

I was assigned a caseworker, Margie. While my daughter and I lived in the women's shelter, my routine was, I would go to work, go to school for six hours, and then go back to my room at the shelter. I had a few days off from work, but I was still going to school. I was only getting about three hours of sleep, but I needed to keep busy. Every day I was riding the city bus. It was getting close to Christmas and it's hard to explain to an eight-year-old that Santa might not come this year. It was depressing to even contemplate. I didn't know what I would do for my daughter's Christmas. My caseworker, Margie, came to my room at the shelter. My daughter was watching a movie with other children in the room.

"You've only been coming out of your room for school and work. Are you okay?" she asked.

"Yeah, I'm fine." I kept my head down when I answered.

"Well Karla, you don't seem fine. What's wrong?"

It took her a few minutes to get me to talk. She hugged me after I told her how guilty I felt. I had ripped apart my daughter's world. At the same time, I knew I had needed to change things. Margie sat me down to talk. She said it was normal to feel guilty for leaving. She asked me if I had thought about going back. I told her, honestly, that the answer was yes. Things were so hard. It was difficult working and going to school. It was difficult getting only a few hours of sleep. So, yes, I thought about it. I knew in my heart and mind that I couldn't go back to him. Every time I thought about going back, I remembered what the doctor had said to me. I remembered the battered girl in the morgue. Margie tried to encourage me to hang in there and be brave. Inside, I didn't feel very brave, but I kept these feelings to myself. Margie told me not to worry about Christmas. The shelter would have a Christmas party for the kids.

At first, I was surprised that the women's shelter was so full in December, but as more women came to the shelter, the thought came to me that Christmas time is "beating season." In a way it really was. Maybe it's the stress of the holiday, the pressure to provide extras that they can't afford. All the ladies who came to the shelter had their own stories of abuse and hearing them affected me. I think it helped me be more determined to not go back. My church took up a collection for gifts for my daughter and me. I was very grateful to them.

I had prayed and told God that I felt selfish to ask for gifts for my daughter. But I realize it is only human to want these things for our children. God humbled me. I had lost everything. When I came to the shelter, all my daughter and I had was the clothes on our backs. I didn't have anything. The shelter gave me toiletries, underwear; the things that most of us take for granted. I was so grateful for everything that the church and the women's shelter gave us. I was grateful, too, for Welfare and Medicaid. My nerves, however, were shot.

I got a letter in the mail. One of the requirements for getting the help from the state welfare office was getting Roy to pay child support. The letter was a reminder that I needed to take my daughter to the health department for a DNA test. This was to prove that Roy was the father in case he protested paying child support. I knew that Roy was her father, but I did what the state asked me to do. I was so nervous about possibly running into Roy, because he also needed to do a DNA test. I was still in so much fear. I was scared to death of him. He had threatened me so many times. He had always told me he would take our daughter away from me. That threat played over and over in my head like a record. Every time I went out, I was looking over my shoulder.

The thought occurred to me that he might be less angry if I called him and asked if he wanted to see his daughter. He was so full of anger talking to me on the phone, but he said he did want to see his daughter. He wanted to meet at the mall. My counselor said it wasn't a good idea, but I wanted him to see his daughter, and for her to visit with her dad. I felt guilty and it was December. Victoria and I rode the city bus to the mall. I was so scared, but I didn't want Roy to see my fear. I didn't want him to think that he could still control me.

I tried to not let Victoria see my fear and anxiety. I smiled at her. She looked at me and said, "Mommy, it will be okay." She squeezed my hand. My child was trying to comfort and reassure me. So many thoughts ran through my head.

On the city bus, I prayed. "Lord, what have I done? I have ripped apart her world. I have destroyed her family. But you know, Lord, I had to get out of the relationship. It was so abusive and toxic." These were the kinds of things that ran through my mind.

I had my hand on my cell phone in my pocket. It wasn't hooked up but the ladies in the women's shelter told me that all cell phones, even old ones with no paid cell phone service, will work for 911. I had never known that before. That knowledge was comforting.

I recognized Roy's Jeep as he pulled up in the parking lot. I prayed for God to give me strength and keep my daughter and me safe. She walked up to her father and hugged him.

"Little Buddy, how are you? Your daddy has missed you." Over her shoulder, Roy gave me a cold stare like he wanted to kill me. I just said hi to him.

Then Roy said for me to get in the car. I did and told my daughter to buckle up. We both buckled up like we always did. He started talking about why I left him, giving me a big guilt trip.

"Well, I guess I was so bad for you that you had to take my daughter and leave," he said. He started driving faster, weaving in and out of traffic. I became more nervous. He was scaring me, and he knew it.

"I don't think now is the time to talk about it," I said, knowing that Victoria could hear our discussion.

"How would you like it if I took our daughter and ran away from you?" he said. He suddenly slammed on the brakes. It scared me so bad. I started praying hard. My heart was pounding. He grabbed my wrist and he bit down on the cigarette he was smoking.

"Would you like that?" He almost whispered as he squeezed my wrist hard.

"No, I wouldn't like it."

Then, he started back in on me. "Women like you make men go

postal." I knew what he was saying.

Victoria was frightened. "Daddy, why did you slam on the brakes?"

He lied and told her a dog ran out in front of the car. I didn't dare say anything different.

"You better not file for child-support on me. You chose to leave me. I am not paying you, Bitch. Not one dime. You bitches are all the same."

"Where are we going?" I asked him.

He said, "Christmas shopping." I told him that the big discount store was a cheaper place to shop.

"That's not good enough for my daughter. We are going to the mall." Roy was still driving like Batman.

I kept praying, "Please, Lord. I won't get in the car with him, ever again. Please, just keep us safe."

Then, his mood suddenly changed to gentleness. "Honey, looks like we are here."

I was thinking, "How can I get Victoria away from him safely?" Earlier, I had given my daughter a cell phone with two hours of minutes on it. I had told her to use it in an emergency; to use it for calling 911. And, we had a code for her to call my cell phone and say the code word. This would tell me that something was wrong.

I asked Victoria if she needed to go to the bathroom.

"Yes, Mommy, I have to go." We both got out of the Jeep and we walked into the ladies' room. I went into the same stall with Victoria and got close to her ear and almost whispered to her.

"Honey, I want you to remember our special word. If I say the words 'Powder Puff Girls,' that is our safety word. If you get scared, we will leave. And if I say the code words, then that means I want you to dial 911 on your cell phone. It means I need help."

"Mommy, will Daddy hurt us?"

"I don't really know for sure. But that's our safety word. Never tell anyone our safety word."

"Okay," she said.

Roy was waiting for us when we walked out of the bathroom.

"What were you two doing in the bathroom so long? Planning an escape?"

"No," I giggled nervously.

"What store do you want to go to, Little Buddy?" he asked Victoria. He picked her up and carried her through the mall. I was almost in a panic, watching his every move. After a while, he put her down so she could walk around.

"Pick out anything you want, Little Buddy." I hated it when he called her that, and he knew I hated it. He treated her like his little friend. He didn't treat her like a daughter, but like a friend his own age.

I kept looking around for all the security cameras. I was also looking for places to hide in the mall, just in case I had to take Victoria and run and hide. When you're leaving an abuser, you can't always predict their actions. I was looking and trying to walk in the view of the security cameras. This was in case something bad happened. I wanted to make a record of where I was with Roy. I know it may seem crazy, but I was on automatic survival mode. I didn't know what his plans were, but I knew I had to make sure that people in the mall saw me.

He was pushing my every button. I had to keep it all cool. I didn't want him to see my fear. However, it was like he could see fear in my eyes. He would look at me and smile an evil smile.

In the meantime, Victoria looked at me. "I don't know what to pick out," she said.

"You like Barbie dolls. Go down the aisle and see what pretty Barbies they have."

I wondered if Roy had a gun in his boots. I knew he owned a gun. I also knew that the gun numbers were scratched off so the gun couldn't be traced. This is one other thing to worry about; if they have a gun, they might use it on you. I couldn't wait to get this visit over with.

"Money is no object. Anything for my Little Buddy," Roy was saying.

Victoria was looking to me like she was asking if it was okay. I told her, "That means he wants you to get anything you want."

She looked for a while and brought back a few things. Then she asked, "Can I get something for Mommy?"

"No," came the response. "She doesn't deserve anything from Santa. Now go pick out more gifts for you."

I knew it wasn't right to tell her, "Rack it up. Get more toys," but I was trying to keep them happy and in a good mood.

His mood was turning darker. I was still watching the time. As we watched Victoria pick out gifts, Roy was telling me in a low voice, "I know you're going to file for child-support."

I didn't say anything.

"You know you make me so mad. I just want to kill your sorry ass."

Then I looked into his eyes. They were full of rage. I didn't know what to say. Anything that I said could set him off. Once again, I looked around for store cameras so that I could be in front of the camera if something happened, or if he hit me. I was seriously in fear for my life. I just wanted to get my daughter and myself out of the store alive.

His mood started to change again. "You know, it's cheaper to just give you what you want," he said.

"What is it that you think I want?" I asked.

"Marriage." He was getting quiet. I didn't know what he was about to do. He dropped down on one knee.

"It's better to keep you in my life than to pay child-support. Will you marry me?"

"People in hell want ice water, too. No!" I said. I knew me getting brass with him and mouthing off wasn't a wise thing for me to do. I instantly regretted it. At the same time, it felt good to tell him just what I thought. I knew that I had to be careful about what I was saying because he could hurt me, or Victoria.

"I told you, it's cheaper to keep you in my life." He whispered, "Women like you do disappear, you know. It would be a shame if that happened to you."

A lady passing by had heard my rude response to him. She said,

"You are some bitch, lady."

I looked at her and said, "Lady, you don't know this man like I do. But he's single and you can have him if you want him."

He smiled at the lady.

"What is behind this? Suddenly you want to get married now? You had 20 years to marry me and now it's just too late," I don't know where I got the words or the courage to say that to him. But I said it. I meant it. I told him, "You don't even have a ring."

He said, "You don't deserve a ring."

Victoria came up with a cart full of toys. I asked her, "Did you get all you want, Victoria?"

"Yes, Mommy."

"I told you, honey, get everything you want," he said to her.

I whispered, "Get everything you want. Roy says it's okay."

She skipped off to get more toys.

"Boy, you know, you are the biggest bitch I've ever known. The state is trying to stick child-support up my ass. No woman is going to get that out of me."

I was still in fear. I told him, "We need to wrap this up soon. I have to be able to get the last bus home."

"That's what you get for leaving me. Now you get to ride the city bus like a loser. How can you subject my daughter to riding the city bus? That's for white trash."
 "Daddy, I've got all I wanted in toys."

"Okay, let's go pay for them," he said.

I looked at the time again. She had picked out $80 worth of toys. I was glad to see this visit from hell winding down. My fears had calmed down a little because the visit was going to end soon. I just kept praying all the way.

"Where do you want me to drop you off?" Roy asked.

"At the city bus terminal." That is where I needed to be dropped off because I couldn't drive.

"Daddy, can I open my gifts when we get home?"

"Yes, honey. Open them all up when you get home."

We got back into his Jeep and once again he was driving fast and weaving in and out of traffic. I prayed for us to get to the bus terminal quickly.

When he left, I told Victoria we would take a different way home. We sat down at the back of the bus. I looked out the back window of the bus and I could see that he was following us to see where we were going. I didn't dare take a chance on going straight home.

We got off the bus downtown and went into the big discount store to wait until my friend, Diana, got off work. She told me that Roy was following me in the store. She told me to go upstairs and stay in the break room until she got off work. Roy couldn't go up there. We ran upstairs where I knew we would be safe. He went through the store looking for us, but finally left. Diana came upstairs.

"Your ex is gone."

Victoria hadn't really known why we went upstairs. She was playing with her new toys. We had to wait until Diana got off work for her to take us home.

"What happened?" she asked me.

I told her how the visit went. I finally calmed down after we got home. I would never do that again. Never, ever, was I going to get into a car with Roy. I was thanking God that we were safe.

- NINE -

Overwhelmed

There was so much I had to do. Getting on my feet was hard. I was in the women's domestic violence shelter for five months. I was a mess and going to counseling. I was diagnosed with post-traumatic stress disorder. I was on antidepressants. I was just trying my best to keep it all together. I kept going to church. I asked God to please help. I needed to do so many things. My problem was that I didn't know how or where to start.

Finding an apartment that I could afford was hard. I found a small apartment but, of course, it was in a bad neighborhood. I was scared living in the apartment alone, just Victoria and me. I had never been on my own. I had never depended on my own self to pay all the bills. It was only me who had to do it all. I didn't have much. Victoria and I had a few clothes, thanks to the women's shelter.

At the shelter, they helped me get on welfare. I started going to school. There were so many things that I didn't know how to do. I didn't know how to write checks to pay my bills. I got a job working at a motel, cleaning rooms. I felt ashamed because I had wasted my life depending on a man. I felt like I was nothing but a failure as a woman and a mother. I would pray so hard and cry. I would beg God to please help me. I met so many people on my life's path. Some of them were helpful and some of them took advantage of me.

I had a good friend, Kathy, but pride kept me from letting her know just how bad things really were. She was a good friend, but she could also be cruel with her words and sometimes that would hurt me deeply. She would have to really make me mad before I could, or would, tell her that she had hurt me with her words. She didn't understand why I was so easily hurt. My emotions were all over the place with how I felt. The fact was, I was so stressed out with everything, just trying to survive.

It had been almost a year since I left Roy. We had done the DNA tests. I received a letter that we would be going to court for child-support. I had mixed feelings about this. I had tried to get Roy to come and see his daughter, but he wouldn't. Roy let me know I had all the control and that this was all my game. I got the DNA papers establishing paternity. I knew Roy was the father of Victoria. The state, however, required this of everyone who sought help from the state.

I had met a guy who was really nice. I will call him Andy. Andy was a good Christian man. I had tried to fake what I did know and what I didn't know. In his friendship, he never shamed me, although he could see my pain. I had called him and was talking to him about how I had to face Roy in court. I was so full of questions and I wanted help from Andy. I didn't know how I was supposed to speak to the judge. I didn't want to sound stupid in court.

Andy really understood what I was asking. He coached me and helped me to speak without an accent. My own accent was deeply Southern. He told me he knew that my southern accent was faked, but that he knew why I used the fake accent and "played stupid." Andy told me I was more than just a dumb blonde. I didn't believe him. My self-esteem was through the floor. I had none. The thing he didn't know was that I was not faking my accent or playing at being stupid, and I was too ashamed to tell him.

Andy judged me because he didn't know all about me. I had been so sheltered and controlled by Roy that there was just so much that I didn't know about life or about managing a household. And my Dyslexia made it hard for me to even pay my bills.

I had other so-called friends putting me down for getting help from the state. They said I was becoming a "welfare mother." As women, we must find compassion for mothers raising their children without any support. I had to feed my daughter while making only minimum wage. Minimum wage doesn't cover everything. Unless you, as a mother, can feed your children without the help of a man's paycheck, please do not judge us "welfare mothers."

What else could I do to feed my child and provide for her with my lack of education and my learning disability? Put yourself in my shoes. Please don't judge anyone using food stamps or getting welfare. It is easy to judge and point your fingers when you have a good job or two incomes.

It was hard to deal with all that I had to deal with. I had no money, little education, a learning disability, and very few friends. Imagine facing the world like that. If you could truly see things through my eyes you might think differently. I tried not to let the criticisms bother me, because I knew I was trying to take care of my daughter, doing the best I could. I was also trying to get my education so that I could support Victoria and myself.

If I could have turned back time, I would have stayed in school and graduated high school. But we all make choices in life. I couldn't change yesterday. I just had to make the best of my situation now. I knew I just had to live for what I did today. And I also knew that I was working hard to make my life and my daughter's life better. Getting my education and getting a better paying job were my priorities. That was something.

Even in our modern times, I think many people don't realize that women do not get paid the same as their male counterparts in the workforce. Because of this, single women tend to stay in poverty.

We need to change some of the laws so women are paid the same as men. I have known women who will marry a man for his paycheck. When a woman tries to leave and be on her own, it seems nearly impossible. You have to take care of your family, especially if you have young ones. But you also have to work outside the home.

Every year it was difficult to pay for Victoria's school supplies, or even her school uniforms. One year, Roy wouldn't help me pay for them. I called him asking for money for these things, but he would always make it about him. He didn't trust me with giving me child-support. He said he didn't trust me with money. So, I suggested that he take her shopping and get the school supplies.

Victoria went to public schools, but the school's policy changed to require all students to wear uniforms until they got into high school. I just didn't have enough money for all my daughter's needs, even though I got her on free lunch. I did everything I needed to do to help my daughter get everything she needed for school. It wasn't easy paying bills on minimum wage. I didn't have much in my little apartment. We had slept on the floor when we didn't have beds, until the church got beds for us, and some household items. I was so grateful to the church for their help.

I grew tired of asking Roy for help. It was always an argument. He would just give me grief about leaving him. He would make it all about him. He was having a pity party for himself. I had long ago lost faith in that man. But I had not lost faith in God. I knew with God's help we would make it.

I had a good friend named Vickie, but every time I told her what all is going on with Roy and child-support, she thought I was mismanaging my money. She had a way of making me feel like nothing I ever did was right. One day she and I really got into it. She kept pressing me on how I wasn't making the best use of the money I had. I felt like she was putting me down because I couldn't make ends meet. I took two quarters out of my pocket and I held them out to her and said, "See these?"

She said, "Okay, you have two quarters."

"Turn them over," I said. She noticed that the quarters were painted red on one side.

"I have held on to these quarters for months. That is my phone call money. If I have to call you, you know I go to the pay phone and let the phone ring twice, then I hang up, and then you call me back. That's the way I have to think about money. Every penny is priceless."

I look at people differently now. When I see women using food stamps or welfare, I do not judge them. What I went through has taught me not to judge anyone. I hope not, but one day, you may have to walk the journey that the lady on welfare is walking. And like us, you will choose to do what's right for your children. If you have to get food stamps to feed them, you will do it. No one knows what you're going through in your life. Unless you are walking the same path as the woman using welfare to feed her kids, then don't ever judge her.

Life has also taught me a lot about people. Sometimes people try to help you and they mean well, but in the end we all have to make our own life choices, even when our friends don't agree with us. I prayed every day that God would help me make it. And He did. But I would say that we all need a little more compassion for and from our fellow men and women.

- TEN -

Dear Daddy

Sometimes we don't see how divorce, or a broken family, or domestic violence affects our children. We don't always see the children's pain. We may think they aren't aware, but they have scars deep inside, just like us. Today, when I watch the home movies that I made of Victoria playing in the bathtub when she was two years old, I can hear her saying, as she is playing, "Don't cry, Mommy. Please don't cry."

On that particular day, in the film, I wasn't crying. I was laughing at some of the things she was saying. At two years old she didn't know the difference. But she was saying to me in a clear voice, "Oh Mommy, please don't cry. I love you, Mommy."

Seeing that home movie of my daughter consoling me, made me realize the impact that her father's abuse of me had caused. At two years old she knew that her daddy had made her mommy cry. She had heard me crying in the night. In one of the movies I had taped of her, she put her hand on her hip and told her daddy, "Don't you dare be mean to my mommy. Don't you make her cry."

Even at the tender age of two, she knew things I didn't dream she knew. At the age of two she asked, "Why does daddy make you cry in the shower?" Her question shocked me. When I asked her what did she mean, she told me that she had heard her daddy and me fighting. I thought I had hidden that from her.

I would cry in the shower because I thought that the sound from the water would drown out my crying. It hadn't even occurred to me that my daughter heard me crying in the shower and crying many times at night. Children don't forget the sounds of their mommy crying.

Don't ever forget to listen to your children. They can tell you more than you think. I know that we, as parents, are not perfect. Most of us have less-than-perfect lives. But nobody should live in abuse. When we continue to live in abuse, we are potentially passing the cycle on to our children.

When you leave an abusive relationship, it is important to get the healing started as soon as possible. The sooner we get out of abuse, the sooner we leave the situation, the better the hope of breaking the cycle. Just as you need counseling, the children will need counseling to understand what's going on in the family. It does our children a disservice if we think that because they are young, they will forget. The damage of seeing their mommy getting beaten really affects the children. Since they are so young, they don't have the same emotional coping mechanisms that we do. They may begin to act out the violence that they see in their fathers. Sometimes children will start fighting at school. Often, one of the early signs of their pain is that their grades start to slip.

The son that sees his mother get hit by the father, may think it is okay, and he hits his mother, too. This is what we teach our sons by staying in the abuse. When we finally leave, we empower our daughters not to accept abuse. We empower our sons to know that they don't have to adopt this as their way of life. We can begin to teach our children what the real meaning of love is.

When Victoria was eight years old, she wrote this letter to her birth father:

Dear Daddy,
Why do you hit mommy? Don't you love her? Why does mommy

cry in the shower? Why daddy, does Mommy hide her eyes with dark sunglasses? Mommy always says she's got to look pretty and the sun is so bright it hurts her eyes. Daddy, I've seen Mommy without her sunglasses, and she's got dark colors. Under her pretty blue eyes the colors are sometimes dark too, with yellow. Daddy, why does she cry so much? Why Daddy, do you yell at her for not cooking your food right?

Daddy, why do you not come see me? Have I been bad, Daddy? Did I do something to make you not love me too? Do you not love me too because I got part of Mommy? Have you forgotten that I'm a little girl? Don't you love me anymore? Why did mommy have headaches? Daddy don't you love me anymore? Daddy, don't hate Mommy because she left you. You were mean to her.

Love you,
Victoria

My daughter wrote this after I had left Roy. Victoria was eight years old. I have a school picture that was taken shortly after we moved into the women's shelter and to this very day, looking at it brings me to tears. The picture haunts me. I see the pain in her little eyes. It still rips my heart out. I knew the pain that I had caused her by staying with her abusive father. I also see in her eyes where I destroyed her world by leaving her daddy. But I had to leave him for her safety and mine. One day, I know God will heal me of this pain of seeing this picture of my daughter. One day God will heal me from the guilt and shame I still hold in my heart and soul.

I can hear God telling me to forgive myself. I pray God will help me to forgive myself. I don't like the thought that I have caused my little Victoria pain.

I included Victoria's letter because I want everyone to understand the hell that children suffer when their mothers stay with a man that hits them. We must think about what our children see. We must understand the pain in their hearts as they watch their mom get hit, or shoved, or slapped.

I didn't always see the pain in her little blue eyes. I didn't always see that she didn't understand what was going on. The world that I created with her father was a world full of fights. It was hell for both of us. It wasn't all hell. There were some good times. But the good times couldn't cover the pain or excuse it.

After I left, Victoria felt her father wanted nothing to do with her. I am still appalled at the things he did to her, mentally and emotionally. Roy never hit her, but from the minute she was born he was never there for her emotionally. Roy didn't go to her plays, even though she asked him to. He would drink his beer and make his excuses. He would tell her that he had to work. I knew the truth was that he just preferred to sit and drink.

I will never forget her pre-kindergarten graduation at church. We drove up in our car. Roy drove and he was drinking a six-pack of beer in the church parking lot. I begged him to come inside and see her graduate.

"I don't do crowds," he said. I wanted to cry. I hid my tears with my smile and my pink sunglasses.

I decided that I was going to make the best of it anyway. I smiled at my little ladybug and said, "Well, I'm here. I have my camcorder and I'm going to take your picture. And we're going to have a good time." I bent down and kissed her cheek and told her I was proud of my big girl. This was in 1999.

Roy always had something more important to do than things with Victoria. I could see by his actions that he didn't want to be a part of her life. And I believe I'm correct in saying that Roy's actions screamed that he didn't want to be a father or a parent. There was no changing Roy. Roy was who he was. His actions spoke for him. It was as if he thought he was a father simply because he had produced a baby.

I think many people see being a parent as just the act of making a baby. Parenthood is a huge undertaking. It takes so much more to be a mom or a dad. So I consoled Victoria that day. I told her not to worry because we would take lots of pictures to show daddy how well she had done.

Victoria was such a beautiful child. The sun would shine on her blonde locks. Anyone would be proud of her. I can still recall her spinning around in her dress, looking like a princess, and asking, "How do I look, Mommy?" She had lacy little socks and little white sandals. She was just a pretty little baby doll. I told her, "Just perfect."

She took my hand and told me to hold her hand so I wouldn't get lost in church. She led the way. I put Roy out of my mind. I didn't want to think about him drinking in the church parking lot. The thought made me so mad, but focusing on Victoria was more important. This was my baby girl's big day! She was graduating her pre-K and she would soon be going to elementary school. I told her to go with the church ladies so that they could get her ready for the show.

Victoria was the announcer. As I kissed her on the head, I told her to sing really loud so that mommy could hear her. I called her my ladybug.

She said, "I will, Mommy. You will hear me." She went back with the ladies.

Roy just didn't want any part of being at Victoria's pre-K graduation. At the time, it showed who he really was. But I still couldn't see it. I held out hope. I wanted so badly for things to work out.

I sat near the front so that I could tape the show and take pictures. The curtain opened up. The children all sat down. Victoria stepped out on the stage.
"Ladies and gentlemen..." then she spoke about the show and the song that they were going to sing.

I thought, "Wow!" She sounded like such a big girl. I took pictures as tears of joy and pride ran down my cheeks. I would switch between taking pictures and taking video of the show. They started singing the song, "One Little Speckled Frog." Victoria was singing so loud that all the parents in the church could hear her. I was giggling. It was so cute. She was out of tune, but it didn't matter. She did so well. I was proud of her and she didn't miss a line.

Afterwards, the children did a song in sign language. It was so darling to watch the little ones singing with their fingers. I am so glad that I never missed a play that my daughter performed in. Those memories will always be in my heart.

I can see things so clearly now, so many years later. Roy was just who he was. I had to accept that. I don't understand to this day why he couldn't change. It is so sad to think about all the things Roy has missed. He never had the joy of being a part of her life. He will never walk her down the aisle. He didn't attend her high school graduation. But I don't dwell on it.

When Victoria was in kindergarten, she met my friend Ms. Charlotte. We found out that Charlotte had cancer. I had a daily routine of walking Victoria to the bus stop.

On one particular day I was telling Victoria that Ms. Charlotte would probably lose her hair due to chemo treatments. I explained it as best I could because Victoria was so young. I knew she wouldn't understand everything.

After school we walked over to Ms. Charlotte's house to see how she was. Her head was shaved. Victoria walked over to Ms. Charlotte and hugged her.

Victoria asked if she could cut her hair and give it to Ms. Charlotte.

Ms. Charlotte laughed and explained that Victoria didn't have to do that because she had a wig. Victoria had a big heart, and she didn't want anyone laughing at Ms. Charlotte because she didn't have any hair. What a lovely thing for little child to want to give of herself. How sad it was for her father to not know this wonderful child.

Even as Victoria grew older, she wanted to cut her hair and give it to children who had cancer. She begged me to let her do this. She grew out her hair and donated it to Wigs for Children in Ohio. They wrote us back to say that her hair had made wigs. I have a picture of how long her hair was before it was cut. Before the attack on the World Trade Center on September 11, 2001, Victoria was going to be featured on Tampa Bay TV on a segment called, "What's Right with Tampa Bay's Kids." Then, the 9/11 disaster struck, and they scrapped her segment.

Karla Reeves

- ELEVEN -

Homeless with My Daughter

After I'd been at the Women's Shelter for almost seven months, I got what I called my "walking papers." What it meant was that the shelter gave me notice that I had to move. Shelters are places that rescue you when you are in crisis; they are not for permanent living. The idea of leaving that safe haven was so scary.

I went looking for a place to live. Several places that I looked at didn't want kids, and the nicer ones cost too much. I was still having daily panic attacks. It was all on my shoulders. I had to figure out a place to live and Roy wouldn't pay me child-support. He would not help me with getting school supplies or uniforms. I was scraping up every dime that I could get.

The school that I was attending would give us bus tickets to help us with riding in the city. I found a listing for a small apartment for $380 a month. They wanted the first month's rent and the last month's rent. I went to look at the place. It was in the "projects" which was a really bad part of town.

I had only a week left to move out of the shelter. The apartment's bedroom carpet had cigarette burns all over it. The wires had been stripped and someone had cut all the wires to the light switches. The place was a mess.

There was a bedroom, kitchen, bathroom and living room. The place was really small, but it was the best I could do. It would be our home. We didn't have much, but we would be off the streets and I wouldn't lose my daughter.

I asked the manager if he could fix the light switches and do something to the carpet. Within the next few days, I would show Victoria our new home. When we moved in the carpet was still wet from getting dyed. I would make the best of the small place. I was so grateful to God for that little place.

I didn't have any place else to go. I didn't have any family that I could move in with. My ex-landlady tried to get me to move in with her, but I had to say no. I couldn't move in with her because it was next door to Roy. Her husband wasn't like Roy. I had to make her understand that Roy was full of anger. She and her husband were often gone out on the road driving trucks. I wouldn't be safe if Roy knew where I was. I knew that he would beat me or have someone else do it and then take Victoria. He had promised to do that if I ever left him. Moving in with her would put her in jeopardy, too. I didn't want to do that. I didn't trust Roy.

We moved into that little apartment with some help from my friends. For the first few months we didn't have beds, so we slept on the floor. We made the best of it. I invited my best friend over and she could see that we didn't have much of anything, so she told the church. The church was so good to us. They got beds for both of us. They also gave us a couch and some other household things. I was so grateful. God had heard my prayers. I thanked God so much for all He had blessed me with. God had supplied our every need.

As I said before, the neighborhood was a bad one. The police were in the apartment complex every day. On the weekends they were there three or four times a day. I worked my new job down the street, only a few blocks from our little apartment. Victoria would ride the school bus home and it arrived at three o'clock. I didn't get home until three-thirty. I always told her if she needed me to call me. I also told her to keep the door locked. She was to answer it for no one. She was to do her homework in the bedroom and if she wanted to, she could watch TV. Our TV was black-and-white and didn't get many TV channels. It did get the local channels. I was happy to have a television for her to see cartoons, which she looked forward to doing on the weekend.

My friend let me wash our clothes at her house to keep me from spending any more money. I did my best with what I had. Everything had to stretch. I worked at the local motel. It wasn't the best paying job, but I got paid every week.

I was so unprepared to manage a household. I opened a bank account for the first time. I was so proud of it. I tried to make my check go as far as I could. I got on food stamps, Welfare, and Medicaid for both of us. It was the best I could do for my daughter and myself.

I didn't feel as if I had anyone to go to for help. I didn't have very many friends and my family was in a different state. I also didn't have a lot of choices about where to live with my daughter. I tried to get relocation money from the state so that I could move back home to Kentucky. Sadly, that didn't work out.

I really wanted that relocation money. It was $5,000. There were a lot of rules to get it. I would've stood on my head if it meant for me to get it. I prayed and prayed so hard. It was quite a letdown for me when I didn't get it. A dear friend told me, "Karla, if God doesn't want you to move out of the state, the door will slam shut. The door that God wants you to go through will open so wide. For every door God slams, other doors will open."

I got depressed about it. I really wanted that door open. I cried about it. I knew what she said was the truth, but sometimes it hurts to hear the truth. Sometimes the truth hurts so bad. I got mad at God for a while. I had to ask God for forgiveness for being so childish. I had been praying for 20 years to move back to my home state of Kentucky. I hated living in Florida, so far away from all I'd known. But God had us there for some reason I didn't yet understand.

I wanted to go back to my home state. I didn't like the hurricanes. The Florida heat was unbearable. One night while I was praying, I said, "Okay God, I give up. I guess no matter how much I pray about it, I am not going to live and raise my daughter in my home state."

That was one of the hardest things to do was to give up that dream of returning to Kentucky. But out of that prayer came my miracle. The miracle taught me to pray with all my heart and then give the prayer to God and believe. I just had to let it go and believe. It would take a little longer. God taught me that it will not be done as Karla willed it, but as God willed it. Sometimes that's the hardest of life's lessons to take in and learn. I felt like I was a kid someone put out in traffic. I had to learn fast.

To say I was in over my head is a gross understatement. I was overwhelmed with things I had to do, and to learn, and decisions that I had to make. If I made the wrong decisions, then we might be homeless again. The stress was so awful. Looking back, it's a wonder I didn't have a nervous breakdown. I did have a support system in my church. I had a few friends, but mostly, I leaned on God.

It was very difficult for me to ask for help. But God humbled me. Eventually, I gave in and asked for help. My pride did nothing but hold me back. Pride was like a noose around my neck, choking me because I couldn't ask for help. I wouldn't ask for help. I had to ask God to show me how to ask for help. It may sound stupid, but I really didn't know how to ask for what I needed. I prayed for God to help me ask for the needs of my daughter and for me.

Things started to change. It wasn't easy. I was just trying too hard to fix things that I could not fix. I had to give in and give it all to God. You know, even as a Christian, for me that was the hardest thing I had to do. I had to just give it all to God and lean on Him fully. People would drive me so crazy. They would say things meant to comfort me. It was like they were patting me on the head saying, "Give it all to God." How do you do that when all you know is how to worry?

My great-grandmother told me that to worry about someone meant that you loved that person. She was a good Christian woman, but I learned that worries don't solve anything. Worrying just gives you the gift of gray hair and ulcers. God began to move in my life and show me more of what I was asking.

It took time, but eventually, I did give it all to God. People made me feel guilty sometimes. Sometimes I felt like I was a bad Christian, because I did worry. It seemed that sometimes I tried too hard. After all, I wasn't perfect. But neither were they. I had to acknowledge that I was only human, and sometimes I did worry.

My brain was spinning with all the decisions I had to make. I kept thinking that if I messed up, I would be homeless. God made me face my biggest fear. Your biggest fear may be something else. For me, in that moment, my biggest fear was being homeless with my daughter. It wasn't easy to face my fears. I had a bag full of them. My fears were weighing me down inside, but I tried to keep it all hidden.

My pride kept me wanting to look like I was strong on the outside. On my inside I was weak and scared. I didn't know what to do. I didn't know who to turn to. I didn't know who to trust. I dug in to God. I prayed and fasted for answers. I confessed my sins and described my failures to him. He showed me so many things. I didn't know how strong I was. He showed me my strength.

Someone had told me that journaling would help me, so I tried to take notes along the way, because I had so many life lessons to learn. I felt like I was falling fast. I had to make the best of it and get God's help.

My life began to change for the better. One of my fears was the fear of making mistakes and falling flat on my face. I didn't have a breakdown. It was like I kept getting hit in the face with challenges, but I kept getting right back up for more of life's lessons. I just couldn't stay down. I couldn't let things defeat me. After all, I had a daughter who needed me. This was God showing me my strength.

But I felt overwhelmed. I had to sink or swim in the ocean of life. Now I can say that God gave me the strength to keep on going. The challenges made me a much stronger woman. I am a new person who knows that with the grace of God I will make it. You will make it, too!

- TWELVE -

I Can't Pay My Bills

I didn't know how to pay bills, literally. I had never had to pay bills. I tried so hard. My last boss at the hotel had been cheating me out of my hours. He wanted us to clock in at 9:00 AM and clean twenty-five rooms and be clocked out by 3:00 PM. I was having panic attacks. I was overwhelmed by all he wanted us to do. I did my best to clean as fast as I could. He was a very demanding and strict boss. He would instruct his wife to come behind me and check my rooms. There were so many things that he wanted done to the rooms. I did my best to get them done as fast as I could. But working as a housekeeper or maid for him was very demanding. I didn't understand how the other ladies were getting finished so much faster. They couldn't possibly be doing all he wanted done in the room. I often tried shortcuts to help me get finished faster. I would have panic attacks so severe that I thought I would be sick. I even tried drinking caffeine drinks to help me move faster in the rooms. But all the caffeine did was make me jittery.

Every day, my boss would fuss at me. He would tell me that I didn't do this or that. I was trying so hard to do everything right. His wife would also fuss at me. They were from another country. Their values were different. I know that not all people from different countries are mean. I realize that just because a person's culture is different doesn't mean that they will belittle or hit women. But this guy had a bad attitude toward women. He certainly didn't like me to challenge him.

I made it clear to him that he wouldn't cheat me out of my paycheck or any hours that I worked. I wasn't taking his abuse. I would report him to the wage and labor board. He told me to get my things and leave. He fired me on the spot.

I knew that the things he was asking all of us to do were unsafe. He was renting his rooms by the hour to junkies, and I knew it. I was going to do something about it. I looked in the phone book and found the number for the wage and labor board. I was going to report him for what he was doing.

That Friday I had to go get my paychecks. He paid us every two weeks. I would have to go back in a week and get my last pay-check, because he paid a week behind. He was in the office when I got there. I could see him through the glass doors. I had made up my mind that I was going to be nice and not say any more than I had to, because he had a temper. His wife was in the office. I walked in and walked up to the counter. I said, "Good morning." His wife looked down at the floor after she asked what I wanted. Then, her husband appeared and asked what did I want and why was I there? I told him in a soft voice that I was there for my pay-check. He said I had no paycheck.

"What?!" I couldn't believe it. I said, "What do you mean, no paycheck? What? You are kidding me."

"No money, now leave." He started walking away. I saw the other maids walking into the office to see what was going on.

I told him, "You have got to be out of your mind. I worked here for my check. You owe me two checks."

"No, you didn't. Now leave my property or I will call the police." He grabbed me.

"Take your hands off me," I said. "This isn't over." I was so mad. But at the time there wasn't much else I could do.

I had kept track of my hours by writing them down. We had time-cards we were supposed to punch in and out when we went to our breaks or out to lunch. There were times I didn't even take my lunch break, because I was trying to get finished with all of my rooms and keep him happy. I even told him I wasn't taking my lunch.

He said, "Okay, work through your lunch." He would punch my timecard himself. He would punch me out at 3:00 PM every day even when I worked until 4:00 PM. He knew I was working an hour over.

Well, I went back home and got my phone book out. I looked up the number for the wage and labor board. Maybe they could help me get my paychecks. I was not going to take this lying down. I found the numbers that I needed, and I filed a complaint. I fought him for my paychecks, but I never did call the police on him for grabbing me.

It took me a long time, but I eventually got my money. I also found another job that same day with a temp agency. I started my new job the next day.

In the meantime, while I was fighting for my money, I couldn't pay my rent or my bills. I was forced to move. I didn't have any-thing of value. I had sold all my rings, but I had only gotten $20 for them. That would not cover my rent. It was not even a drop in the bucket for all the bills I had. I made the mistake of telling my closest friend Vicki about my many problems. I think her husband thought that I was just spending my money wildly. I sat down and wrote out every dime I spent. They asked me about my two pay-checks that I should have had.

I was embarrassed and I didn't want to tell them what had hap-pened, but I found myself trying to defend myself, telling them the whole story. I'd also told them about my marked quarters and how I had clung onto them for so long. I felt like my two friends were thinking that I was wasting my paycheck.

I don't think people understand the mindset of a victim of abuse. I had become so used to being defensive. The truth is that is how and why I was acting like I was. I was not trying to give excuses. I had been trained by Roy to defend my every move. Roy had always asked me to explain myself. If I took a bath at midnight he would question why. It was crazy to have to explain everything like that. Being with Roy for 20 years had just trained me to be defensive.

Roy had wanted me to go to bed when he went, get up when he got up. I couldn't stay up and watch a movie. Until you have walked in the shoes of an abused person, you can't really understand the mental abuse and how it changes how the victim thinks, how they feel, and eventually who they are. The abuser controls every move. The abuser wants to treat the other person as a possession, and they want to destroy their spirit. If they can achieve this, they will make them a mindless victim who simply obeys their every wish. They brainwash their victims into thinking the thoughts they want them to think. If you tell someone for 20 years that they are fat or they are worthless, they will begin to believe it. Roy broke my spirit. I don't think people understand how the abuse affects the victims.

People think you can just leave, and they tell you so. It's not that easy. When people are isolated and fearful, that fear and pattern of being controlled makes them feel helpless.

When I left my parents' home with Roy, at age sixteen, my father told me, "Now you have made your bed. Go lie in it." I was so young and foolish. I had made a mistake. That mistake had caused me to be thrown to the wolves. Now I had to grow up and take care of Victoria and myself. I made up my mind to make it. No matter what life threw at me, I was going to make it. Some people judged me. It is so easy for others to point their fingers in judgment or in gossip. Instead of just saying, "You should just leave," people should ask if you need help to leave the abuse.

I didn't know any better. I didn't even know how to get out. However, I feel like I have walked my life's journey with God. I prayed to God for his wisdom. I prayed for his help to get out. It was always hard for me to ask Him for help. Pride is a deadly sin. The hardest thing I ever had to do was to believe in myself.

I did not get those two paychecks until 2005. I had to fight for the money. I went to a website called Forgotten Money. I filled out the paperwork to get my money that was owed. I still didn't get all the money he owed me. Sometimes you have to fight for what's right. God had humbled me by taking everything. This helped me to see just how very blessed I was. Without God I am nothing, and I certainly couldn't have made it without Him.

Karla Reeves

- THIRTEEN -

Another Kind of Abuse

I got a letter in the mail saying I now had a new caseworker. I always dreaded going into the food stamp office to re-file for benefits. I would rather have had my teeth pulled without any painkillers. I have had that done before, so I know how bad it hurts. I'm using this as an example to talk about how much I dreaded all the hoops that I would have to jump through. It tore up my nerves. I hoped that I would get lucky and get a good caseworker. Some caseworkers acted like they had a chip on their shoulder. I felt like they looked down their nose at me for needing help. Inevitably, there would be a long wait in the office before being called back to see the caseworker.

Another life lesson God taught me was how to be patient. It seemed as if everyone in the room had been booked into the same time slot. The room was packed with kids running around. I observed that sometimes the more wild the child acted, the faster their parents would get pushed through the appointment. I wondered if the mothers told them to show out and act wild to get on everyone's last nerve to get them in and out of the office faster. It was just a thought. I couldn't know for sure.

I couldn't help but smile at the antics of the children. It was so funny. Some of the kids and their parents spoke Spanish. The office workers couldn't speak Spanish to call the children down. The mothers of the children couldn't speak English.

I looked in my little handbag and I had a few pieces of candy. You guessed it; nothing like a sugar rush for the little darlings. Lord, forgive me for doing that, but it was my way of giving a little love back to them.

After waiting for hours, they called my name. I walked up to the desk. The lady told me to follow her. We went way back into the back to a little cubicle. It seemed degrading to tell everything they asked, but I did what they asked me to do. I smiled and pretended that it didn't bother me. My new caseworker, I'll call her Cheryl, shook my hand and I sat down when she told me to. She said there was yet another paper that I needed to fill out.

Unfortunately, it didn't take me long to figure out that she did have a chip on her shoulder. She was like a drill sergeant. She dotted the i's and crossed the T's. She went over the rules one page at a time. I prayed that she would get moved off my case soon. I did manage to get all the paperwork that she needed. She was going through my past paperwork page by page. I could tell she wasn't going to be a fun caseworker. It seemed as though she took her job way too seriously, but I was going to make the best of things.

She said she wanted me to comply with the rules. She informed me that I was one hour short of meeting my requirements for the state in terms of classes. She said, to make it up, I had to write a 500-word essay on what I would do if I were president. She wanted it done in a day. I told her that I would have it on her desk by the next day. She told me that I should come back at lunchtime on the following day. I remember thinking that she was being a little hard on me, but I was determined to do what she asked. So I wrote the essay.

The next day I had to ride the city bus back to her office. When I handed her the essay, she immediately started counting words. I thought, "Good Lord." Word for word, she sat there counting. I told her that I had typed it on the computer and that it counted the words for me. She wouldn't give me a break. She announced that I was short of words and I would have to write another essay. This time my subject would be on how I would change the world. Thank God, I didn't tell her what I was really thinking on the subject matter. I bit my tongue and smiled and said, "Sure, you will have it."

When I went back to school, my teacher, Ms. Gail, could tell that something was wrong. She asked me to tell her what it was.

"My caseworker, Ms. Cheryl, counted my every word on my essay. She said that small words didn't count, which made me short on my word count." I told Ms. Gail that I now had to do another essay and I was going to make it 1000 words long, instead of 500, to be sure to satisfy Ms. Cheryl.

When I turned in my thousand-word essay to Ms. Cheryl, she said that there were far too many misspelled words and she would have to count that against me. I would have to do another essay.

Ms. Gail was surprised when I came in again with another essay assignment. She asked me, "How many does that make this week?"

Another girl in the class overheard us discussing the matter. She said she had the same caseworker and that she was being harassed as well. I asked Ms. Gail if she thought there was anything we could do about this. She agreed with me that it was harassment. She talked to the other teacher, the one who ran the school, and told her that Ms. Cheryl was giving some of us a hard time. We all thought that Ms. Cheryl was abusing her power. Mrs. Brown, who ran the school, said that she would have a talk with Ms. Cheryl's boss. They were good friends.

The next day I was called in to Cheryl's office. I was dreading it. I was wondering what I did wrong this time.

I sat down and Cheryl told me her boss was coming in to talk to us. She explained that I would need to tell her boss that she had been good to me and I should tell her boss how much she had helped me out. I didn't know what to say. It was a lie. Cheryl was daring me to say anything to her boss.

"Someone has been talking to my boss. They said I have been treating the deadbeats in the GED classes bad," she told me. "Now Karla, I know you will tell my boss that I've been really fair and how much I've helped you out, giving you all those extra essays to write. I note that this has helped your writing. You will tell her that, won't you?"

"Sure, I guess," I said.

Soon, her boss, Ms. Maria, walked in. She asked me how Cheryl had treated me during the time she had been my caseworker.

I told her, "Yeah, she has helped me out."

"Has she ever treated you unfairly?" Miss Maria asked.

Cheryl was glaring at me. Her eyes dared me to say a wrong word. I was getting nervous.

Ms. Maria said, "If she's treated you unfairly, Karla, we can give you another caseworker."

I looked at Cheryl who mouthed the words, "Don't you dare."

So I said, "She's fine; she's nice."

I didn't feel right about lying. Her boss seemed satisfied with my answers. She went back to her desk. Then, Cheryl thanked me for saying what she wanted. For the next week, she was really nice to me. I knew this was not genuine kindness and I really couldn't wait until her time was up being my caseworker.

Complaining had gotten me nowhere. I was forced to deal with Cheryl. It felt good for a week not to have homework. No more crazy essays. Cheryl took her advantage of her position and abused her power. I had to make the best of a bad situation. I prayed that her being nice would last a while.

The other girls from my class were still being harassed, too. I felt we had to do something about it. I knew I should have spoken up about how she was treating me. I was in a tough situation. I needed the Medicaid help for my daughter. I needed the food stamps. I was trying to work and get my education to better myself. I was trying to comply with the state's welfare laws but having Cheryl as my caseworker added extra stress.

She would play these little games with me. She'd put her hand on my leg and rub it. She called me "Honey." I felt so uneasy about her. Her harassment had begun to be sexual harassment.

I thought that what I really needed was proof of what she was doing and how she was talking to me. By this time, she had gotten much worse. She was connected, and the people there just seemed to back her. It was my word against her word. This is why I finally made the decision to secretly tape our conversations.

I was taking a risk. I knew she could make my life pure hell if this didn't work. I had to make her stop what she was doing. In the state that I lived in I would be breaking the law by taping her. I couldn't legally tape her unless she knew it and said that it was okay. I just had to stop her abuse. I knew the other girls in my class were also suffering. I wanted to figure out a way to stop it.

Soon, I had another appointment with her. I wasn't looking forward to it. Although the time I spent speaking with my caseworker was only minutes, I always had to wait for hours. Finally, I was called back to her little cubicle. She looked like she was in one of her moods again. I thought, "Oh boy, this won't be fun."

She put her hand on my leg and called me "Honey."

I told her, "My name's not 'Honey,' it's 'Karla.'"

"Now, Karla, you know how I speak. I don't mean anything by it." She was still rubbing my leg. I picked her hand up off my knee and removed it.

I told her, "Please don't touch my leg. It makes me uneasy."

She touched my leg again.

I asked her, "Please, do not touch my leg again." My heart was beginning to race.

She asked, "Why did you turn me in to my boss?"

"I don't like how you are harassing me and being mean. I felt like you were abusing your power with all of those essays."

She looked at me and said, "You know we can work this out, this misunderstanding, don't you?"

"Oh, how can we fix this?" I asked her. I was thinking about getting this all on tape. "How can we fix this?" I asked her again.

She told me I could meet her at the bar on Main Street. She said that I could go home with her a few times. "We can just go out and have a good time, just you and me. This can all be resolved and just go away."

I asked her, "What do you mean, we go to your house?"

She said, "Oh, Karla, I mean you sleep with me." There it was. They couldn't mistake that.

"What if I do tell your boss on you?" I asked, a little too loudly for her taste.

"Lower your voice, please." She said.

"Why?" I asked.

I was getting upset. I was not going to let her force me to date or sleep with her. It didn't matter if she was a man or a woman, it was wrong to sexually harass me. It was wrong, no matter how you look at it. She was abusing her power. I had the right to be treated with respect. I was tired of her walking all over me. I was getting mad, but I knew I had to keep it together.

"If you don't do what I ask, this won't go easy on you," she said.

"Oh, Cheryl," I said, "That sounds like a threat." Again, I spoke loudly.

"Lower your voice," she advised. "People are looking."

She narrowed her eyes and said, "Karla, it is not a threat. It's a promise. I can, with a few keystrokes, make your life a living hell."

"Oh, but that is a threat, Cheryl. You cannot do that."

"Oh, yes I can. I have so much power over you food stamp losers. You don't even have an education. I can do anything I want to you. You can't do a damn thing about it."

By this time, I had more than I needed on her. I stood up and said even louder, "I am turning you in."

Cheryl laughed at me. "Oh, Maria won't do anything to me. We are best friends."

I told her, "We will just see about that." I walked up to Maria, looking at Cheryl who was across the room. I watched Cheryl as I spoke to Maria.

Maria asked me what she could do for me. I told Maria about Cheryl's harassment of me. Maria spoke with me first. After that she called in Cheryl. I repeated myself in front of Cheryl. I told Maria that Cheryl was sexually harassing me. I told Maria the things that Cheryl had said and done. I could tell by the look on Cheryl's face that she was boiling mad. Even so, she talked her way out of things and made me look like a fool.

She said, "Karla, this is a big misunderstanding."

She told her boss, "Karla is a little slow and she mistook my kindness for a come on." Cheryl looked at me. I didn't even smile. She laughed, and then continued, "This is a big misunderstanding."

She managed to smooth things over with her boss. I felt like she made a fool out of me. Even before the meeting was over, Cheryl asked me to see her before I left that day. I was worried. I knew hell had just got a little hotter for me. I went over and sat down at her desk.

Cheryl walked in. "Well, Miss Karla, that didn't get you anywhere, did it?"

"No, Miss Cheryl."

She spoke softly. "Karla, I guess you forgot what I said about how I can make your life a living hell with just a few keystrokes. I can cause all sorts of trouble for your case. You can't prove anything on me except that I was helping you. So, now your life will be pure hell, because I am on your case."

She looked intensely at me. "I will see you first thing Monday at nine a.m. We will fix this mess. Next Friday, you will meet me at the bar, and we will talk this out.

"I will see you at our appointment on Monday," I told her. Before I left, she gave me another essay. By this time, I was getting pretty good at writing them.

I walked out of the office and made my way to the city bus. Sitting on the bus, I was thinking about what I could do. I came back to the thought of taping our conversations. I was forced to do something. I knew I had to somehow stop the abuse.

Monday came and I rode the city bus to the food stamp office. I had my new mini tape recorder. I prayed Cheryl wouldn't harass me again, but if she did, it would be on tape this time.

I got to the office early and I went to the bathroom right before she called me back. I asked God to forgive me for breaking the law by taping her, but I just couldn't allow her to get by with this. She was doing this to several different people, and we all felt helpless to stop her.

I had put black electrical tape over the red light on the mini tape recorder so that the light would not show through my top. I clicked on the "record" button and made sure the volume was turned all the way up. The tape recorder was voice activated. This meant that it only recorded when it picked up voices.

I placed it carefully down in my bra. My heart was pounding so hard. I felt as if the mini recorder was going to pick up my heartbeat above anything else. I pointed the little red light away. Even with the electrical tape, I was afraid Cheryl might see it. I glanced in the mirror before leaving the bathroom to make sure that nothing showed through. I was happy to see that nothing showed. Thank God, I was big-busted.

Even as I had made up my mind to tape Cheryl, I kept hoping that she would act like a professional. If she had, I would not have turned her in. I really didn't like being forced into this extreme. At least if it was caught on tape, I would feel vindicated.

If I thought that the weekend might have cooled her down a bit, I was mistaken. She was as mad as a wet hen.

"What did you think you were doing by telling my boss, Maria, all of that? You said things that weren't true. Well, Sweetie Pie," she began to rub my leg again.

I asked her to take her hand off of my leg.

She said, "Oh, Sweetie, you get more homework essays from me. I guess you thought I was joking when I told you that with a few keystrokes of my fingers I could make your life a living hell."

I looked at her. "Why would you do that?" I asked. "You are abusing your power. You know I need help with medications for my daughter."

"I don't care. Next time you will know that when I promise you something, I mean it."

"I just don't understand. Why are you threatening me?"

"It is my promise to you, remember? I will make your life a living hell. I might send over one of my staff members to investigate the abuse you are doing to your daughter."

I was shocked. "What are you talking about? I am not abusing my daughter."

She was so cold. "Just try me, Karla. I hold your worthless life in my hands," then she laughed. "You forget what all I can do to you. Guess you forgot my promises. I can get your medical benefits taken from you. Forget Food stamps. I can even make sure that your ex-husband gets custody of your daughter."

I was flabbergasted. "You are crazy, Cheryl." I was getting so mad that I just wanted to throw her computer at her. I realized that wouldn't help my cause. I just had to keep my composure and try not to lose my temper. If I did, I would get put in jail and she would look like the victim.

"Now, do you want to rethink dating me?"

"No," I told her. "I am not going out with you. You are sexually harassing me. Stop this! I am not going to take it!" I was raising my voice again.

"Keep your voice down." She advised.

I stood up.

"Where do you think you are going?" Cheryl asked me.

"I am leaving," I told her.

"Oh, are you going to my boss again, Karla? Are you going to go see Maria? She's not going to do anything."

I went to the front desk and asked them where John, the top manager, who was Maria's boss, was.

Afterwards, I went to the bathroom. I went into the stall and took the mini recorder out of my bra. My heart was still pounding, and I remember hoping that the recorder had recorded something other than the sound of my own heartbeat. I was praying that it had picked up everything that she said.

I played it. It got everything. I took a deep breath. "Lord, I've got to do this, just give me the strength I need."

I told the lady at the desk that I needed to speak to John. Cheryl was there, glaring at me. She mouthed the words, "Remember my promise."

After me turning her in the first time, she had put a sanction on my case file.

Maria asked why I needed to speak to John.

I was told that I would be called back in a minute because John was on the phone. Maria asked again, "Why do you need to speak to John?"

"It's a private matter."

Maria said, "If there is anything that you want to talk to me about, you know that you can come to me."

"Yes, thanks," I told her. "I only want to speak to John."

"What is this about?" Maria asked.

"It is a private matter," I repeated.

Cheryl walked up. "This better not be about me again. Remember what I said to you."

Now, it was my turn to smile. I said nothing. They told me to go back to the waiting room. Cheryl grabbed my arm and said, "This complaint will get a black mark on my permanent record. You think about this. Remember my promise."

I looked at Maria and Cheryl, "I have nothing more to say to you."

My nerves were so bad. I had to run to the bathroom and be sick. But I had made up my mind. For once in my life, I wasn't going to get run over. I would not be walked on. I washed me face and hands. I steeled myself. I was going to stop her.

Twenty minutes later the lady at the desk called me saying, "John will see you now."

As I walked in, I thought about Cheryl grabbing my arm. I guess we were going to see about it being my word against hers. I didn't care what she did to me in the future. One thing that was for sure, she wouldn't do this to me again.

"Hello, Karla, I am John. How can I help you?"

I told John that I had already tried to resolve this matter. I told him about Maria and how she had failed to fix the problem. I told him, "I really am sorry that I've had to come to you about this."

"I am being harassed by one of the workers," I said, and I told him that she was also sexually harassing me.

"You know you are making a very serious accusation," he said. I told him that I had proof of the things she was saying. I opened my handbag. I pulled out the recorder and laid it on his desk.

"What's this?" He asked.

"It's the conversation of me and her that I taped. I want to play it for you and see what you think." He took it and clicked "play."

I could see the anger gather in his face.

"Well, I am certainly not happy with what I have heard," he said.

"I apologize for taping her," I said, "but I felt I had to."

He asked me if I had spoken to Maria about this. I told him that I had gone to her before, but nothing had been done to correct the situation and that Cheryl had just continued to behave in this manner.

He told me he would have to look into the matter. He said he was going to have to speak with them. He wanted me to wait in his office. So I did. I was thinking, "Oh, Lord, he's going to bring them down here and this isn't going to be good."

I was right. A few minutes later, in they walked. He told them to sit down. He told both of them that I was complaining about Cheryl mistreating and harassing me.

Cheryl sat up boldly and said, "She's lying."

John asked Maria if she knew anything about this. She said, yes but there was no proof. She said Cheryl was a good caseworker and she had no reason not to believe her over me.

Finally, he picked up the little recorder. I looked at Cheryl's face. It was priceless. You could see her confidence melt as the tape began to play. He told both of them that he had the conversation of her harassing me. He asked Cheryl if she could explain what was on the tape. I watched her expression as her face drained of color. She looked like she was going to pass out.

She stammered. "I was only joking," she said nervously.

He told her there was no reason for her to be unprofessional and threaten me.

She couldn't say, "I am so sorry, Karla," fast enough. She admitted to what she did, and John asked her how she could speak to me the way she did. He told both of them to go back to their desks.

I sat there as they walked out. He apologized to me over and over. I told him that I wanted her stopped, whatever he had to do. I didn't want my caseworker to abuse her power. And abuse is what she did.

I asked him, "Does this office have ethics that the caseworkers are supposed to follow?"

He told me that there were ethics that they were supposed to follow. They were definitely supposed to treat us with respect.

I told him that I never expected to be treated special, but that I did expect to be treated with respect. I told him that I wanted her corrected. I told him that I wanted a new caseworker. I also told him that I was concerned that she might try to make good on her threat to tamper with my records.

He said that he would do something about what happened and that it would not happen ever again. I told him that no government worker should ever treat anyone the way I was treated. Cheryl had been wrong to do that. I had requested another caseworker two months ago and had not been assigned a new one.

I explained to him that the government had rules for me to follow, and that I did my best to follow them. He agreed with me that it did seem like I had tried to follow the rules and seemed to be doing all the things that I was supposed to be doing.

In the end, their investigation revealed that Cheryl had been treating other people in the same manner. They fired her. I got another case worker, and I was treated with respect. John sent me a letter apologizing for all that had happened. He fixed my records from where she had put a sanction on me for stupid reasons. He told me that she had sanctioned me when I was following the rules. He had fired her because of all the things they found out about her.

I worked really hard to get off the welfare system. I worked for minimum wage and it was so hard not getting the child support that I should have been receiving for my daughter. My employer would not give me a full-time position so that I could better take care of my daughter's needs. I did the best I could.

- FOURTEEN -

What Is a Parent?

I knew that after doing the DNA testing, I would be required to file for child-support. I knew this would enrage Roy. In the past, he had told me many times about his ex-wives. He had told me that they wouldn't get any money from him. I didn't really know if his callous attitude was because he was childish or because he really didn't care. I couldn't understand how someone could not care about the well-being of their child.

There are many fathers and mothers who make child support about themselves instead of making it about meeting their children's needs. Anyone can become a parent. The act of having sex can result in a child, but being a real parent means providing for the child's needs, both physical and emotional. Children need food. Children need a safe place to live. And children need love and emotional support, too. It takes so many things to be a good parent. I know most of us do the best we can. Everyone makes mistakes while raising our children. I've learned so much just by having my daughter.

When she was first born, I didn't even know how to change a diaper. I learned through experience the same way many new mothers learn. I bonded with her the day she was born. I always tried to put her first.

Sometimes being a parent means putting yourself last. That was okay with me. If I needed shoes that was fine, but I would make sure she had new shoes first. I didn't always have the money for brand new shoes or fancy brand-name shoes, but Victoria always had what she needed.

I didn't want to put Roy down for all the things he didn't do as a parent. Like I said, we all make mistakes as parents. Neither one of us was perfect. I just felt that Roy's priorities were messed up. All Roy seemed to want to do was drink and work on this race car with his friend.

Roy always told me he couldn't afford to pay child support because his best friend wouldn't pay him. His friend raced and even when he won the race, Roy said he wouldn't give him any of the prize money.

Roy didn't want to be a parent or a husband. He just wanted to come and go as he pleased. He missed out on bonding with his little baby girl. He couldn't understand why every time he tried to hold her when she was little, she would cry. I felt bad that she did this, but the truth was, he was a stranger to her. He had other things in his life that were more important to him.

It's easy to make a baby. It takes a real man or woman to be a parent. Children are a gift from God. To be a parent is more than just being able to breed and make kids. Being a parent is raising a child to be a productive person. It is teaching them to stand on their own feet as an adult.

When I was working, Roy tried to get me to pay his child support on one of his sons from a previous relationship. This upset me for so many reasons. He made the baby; I didn't. Why should I have to take responsibility for a baby that I didn't make? I got so upset with him.

"This is your son," I said. "You made him with your wife. You should stand up and be a man and take responsibility for him."

Then he said, "Well, I caught her in bed with another man. She cheated."

I asked him, "Then what did your son do to you to be punished? It's not about her cheating. It's about your son. Taking care of him, feeding him, clothing him, seeing him, loving him."

Roy couldn't find seven dollars to send his ex-wife for support. I thought it was pretty sad that he thought so little of his little boy that he wouldn't even send him seven dollars. In his mind he was punishing the mother for what she did, by not providing support for his son.

I don't know if his ex had really cheated. I don't even know if it was even half true, and it's not my place to judge her. One day he will probably have his new girlfriend paying the back child-support that he owes for the daughter that he and I made. I already know from experience that he will try to get her to pay his child support.

Parenting means nurturing. A good parent or guardian is always looking out for the needs of the child. A good parent knows their children's clothing sizes. A good parent knows what shots their children have had. A good parent puts their child's needs before their own needs. Parents stay up with children when they're sick.

A good parent will pay child-support on time and without hesitation. It isn't fair for someone to say that the child-support money won't be used for the child. It's expensive to raise a child. Everyone knows that.

Parents who don't pay their child support should be ashamed of themselves. Being a parent is so much more than just being able to bear children. Being a father is so much more than just creating a child.

Roy was so immature. He didn't know how to be a father, and the truth is, he also had no desire to learn how to be a good father. If I had reflected more on his past, I would have realized that Roy walked away from all his children. There was so much that I didn't know about Roy when I fell for his charms. And I didn't get a book of instructions for being a parent. Children don't come with a "how to" book. You learn as you go. I know I'm not a perfect parent. All that I can do is my best.

I have tried to see the world through my daughter's eyes, which has given me a different perspective on life. My child has made me a better person. You are the person that you've always been, but much more defined. You have to create a secure place for your child. Sometimes the child will take on traits of the parents.

When I became a parent, I had all sorts of fears. I suppose all new moms go through that. I think I did just fine. When I think back on my childhood and my parents, I have some good memories and I have some bad ones. We all make different parenting choices. Life isn't easy. As hard as it is for me to say, sometimes being a good parent means walking away from bad situations, so that you won't do damage to your child.

We are constantly learning about life. I've seen people who don't realize how much their children need them. Roy just seemed to never grow up. He missed an opportunity that he will never get back. He tried to be her friend. Sometimes parents have to correct their children with love. We have to teach them right from wrong. One day they will stand on their own. The world is a scary place. There are rules to living in the world, rules that we have to impress upon our children. You teach them all that you can and then you pray for the rest. Being a parent is a twenty-four hour a day, seven days a week job. It is also one of the most rewarding jobs you'll ever do.

Victoria does well in school. She's very smart. But the thing that

I like best about her is that she's very compassionate to others. I had prayed thirteen years for a child. God blessed me with her. Even though all the things I went through with Roy made it difficult, I will always be grateful for our daughter. Even though he didn't want to be a parent, I did. I hope that Roy can live in peace for all the choices he's made.

I can't say that there was no good in Roy. I saw it from time to time. He had issues. In a way he was a broken person. I knew he had it in him to be good. Alcohol influenced his judgment. I don't hate him. I don't wish any ill will on him. I know who he is. I have come to accept the person that he is.

I could not make Roy into a good parent. I used to think that I could change him, but he wasn't ready to change. We can't force change on another person. Only he can answer to why he made the decisions that he did.

Good, bad, or indifferent, Roy was the person that he was. I wish that he could see what he's missed of his daughter's life. I wish this for her sake. She tries to hide how she feels about her biological father, but I can see the pain in her eyes that he has caused. She has a right to feel anger towards him.

I will never discourage her if she wants him in her life. If she loves him and wants a relationship with him, I will never discourage that. I put her needs before mine. I wish that I could have provided more for her. I tried to get her father to pay child-support, even though he had threatened that I would never see a dime.

I have thought many times about his words. He thought he was punishing me. He always thought he was punishing his other ex-wife by not paying child support. But it was his children who were affected most. If I could get a message across it would be that paying child support makes an important difference in the life of your child. If a person doesn't want to be a parent, then let them sign their rights away. Their children deserve a better tomorrow. Your children deserve your best no matter what that might be.

- FIFTEEN -

Another Abuser

Having come so far in my journey, it is hard for me to admit that I moved in with another abuser. I know that I called one of my chapters "The Doctor that Saved My Life." You may be thinking that he didn't change my life very much, since I moved in with another abuser. I remind you not to judge me. I wrote this book to facilitate understanding. I realize that people don't understand the decisions that I've made. And it's not just me that people don't understand. People have a hard time understanding the reason why many women stay in abusive relationships, or get back into bad relationships, after they've finally gotten out.

I am trying to be honest. That doctor did change the way I saw my life. And he certainly changed the way that I looked at my daughter's life. He was impactful on my life. As you read this book, try to place yourself in my shoes.

It was not easy finding good jobs with little education, and very little money. I might be judged harshly by some of the people who read this book. It is scary putting myself out there. I haven't even begun to speak about my learning disability, dyslexia, and how it affected everything I tried to do.

I decided to move in with another man. I try not to make excuses for myself, but in my defense, at the time, I had no idea he was abusive. The truth was I had no family to go to when I lost my apartment. Remember, I had never been out on my own. I had never had to pay my own way. I only had an eleventh-grade education. In fact, when I started my GED classes I started with a third-grade reading level. I was tested and I found out I had a learning disability called dyslexia. To make matters worse, I also had problems with math. I couldn't count numbers. I couldn't see the numbers like other people do. Things that other people take for granted like running a household, paying the bills, writing checks to pay the bills, I simply couldn't do. I was ashamed of not being able to do normal things like other people did. I had to learn to develop special skills in order to overcome my disability.

Looking back on my childhood, it is hard to understand how the teachers passed me along when I didn't understand. I had a twin sister. I saw my teacher copy my grades from my twin sister's report card. One of us didn't get our real grades. The teacher took whichever twin's grades were higher. We always got the same grades.

I was in school from 1968 to 1982. At some point the school system had a program called "No child left behind." While the intent of the program was to make sure that every child got an equal education, in reality, I got passed no matter how my grades really were. It was a real problem. I know now we also had football players coming out of our schools who couldn't read.

When I was in the eighth grade, I was in a class called pre-algebra. I was having real problems in math. I tried explaining it to the teachers. I tried asking my eighth-grade teacher for his help. I told him I wasn't understanding the math. He wasn't very good at explaining things. He was the kind of teacher that told you, "Just read the book and do the math." Even I realized that I was slower than the other kids in class. This particular teacher just couldn't help me.

One day he asked me to do a math problem on the chalkboard. I refused. The students in the class were encouraging me to be disobedient. I wasn't trying to make problems in the class, I just didn't want to be embarrassed. The teacher sent me down to the principal's office. I was put out of the class for being a trouble-maker.

Then the teachers shoved me off to the classes with children who were considered mentally handicapped. I was given math for second graders.

At the time, I didn't understand that I had dyslexia. I don't think my teachers understood my learning disability either. I often received the label of being "slow" or "lazy." This made me crazy. I knew I wasn't lazy. I was telling the truth when I said that I was having a real struggle.

Having dyslexia affects most of my everyday life. There are so many things that most people take for granted -- things like reading signs, getting directions, writing checks, paying bills. Those were all so difficult. I want people to have a full picture of my life before they judge me. Before I tell my story, people have to understand me. I pray you will have a little empathy for me, and the things I did. I felt I had no one but God. Have you ever been there? Have you ever felt that you had no one, no money, no car, nothing?

I have judged myself as a woman and a mother more harshly than anyone else could ever judge me. I know that I have made many mistakes in my life and in raising my daughter. I can say with an open and honest heart that I have done the best I could with the things that I had. Now I pray every day that God shows me how to forgive myself. I can forgive anyone but myself. Forgiving me is the hardest thing I have to do.

My daughter tells me to forgive myself. She tells me that she has forgiven me. She giggles and tells me that she has duct tape, and she can use it on me. She knows how to make me laugh. I pray Victoria never has to make the decisions I've had to make. My daughter will always have a home no matter how old she is, and I make sure to tell her that often. I've lived my own personal hell. I don't want her to go through what I did.

I have told you the story about the man that I worked for at the hotel. The next job that I had was at a telemarketing company. Eventually, that company was raided by the police for credit card fraud.

I had only been making $6.15 an hour, which wasn't enough to pay all my bills. I had a light bill, a water bill, a gas bill, bus tickets, lunch money for Victoria to eat at school, and I had to buy school uniforms. The telemarketing company had required me to wear suits. I bought two cheap suits that would mix-and-match with each other. I bought one all-black suit with the jacket for $15 and the other one was a tan color to mix the jacket with the other skirt. This made me have a few days-worth of nice clothes to wear. I bought black shoes so they would go with anything.

The secondhand store where I shopped was in a nice part of town, so they had really nice clothes. The church I went to had a thrift store and clothes shop and they gave out food for the needy. I would volunteer my time in exchange for an outfit for my job. I chose a dark navy-blue blazer and white pants. I got the basic colors like blue, white, and black. I chose solid colors. I knew they would all match my other suits so that it looked like I had more suits than I really had. I only had four suits in total. I made different suits out of the colors by mixing and changing the jackets. At the church shop, I saw a blazer that was dark pink. I thought, "Wow."

It was so pretty. I tried it on. I put it back on the hangar. I thought, "I just needed a few suits. I didn't need to get something just because it was pretty and pink."

The church lady that ran the place came up to me and said, "Karla, why did you put the jacket back?" I told her that I had enough suits for my office job. She said for me to put it back on so that she could see how it looked on me.

She said, "Karla that looks nice on you, why don't you take it, too?"

I told her, "I just can't. I know there are other people that need things, too. I would feel selfish if I took the pink jacket as well as the other things."

She told me, "Karla, you deserve it. Please take it."

I looked down at the floor. She hugged me and told me it was okay. She said they get more like it every day.

"It would be a shame for you not to take it," she said. "It looks so pretty on you."

I told her that they have so many people that are so much more needy than me. I felt like that I couldn't take the jacket.

She said, "Well, okay then, bring up to the counter what you have."

She saw that I only had a few outfits. I had picked some clothes for Victoria. She placed the pink jacket in my bag. "Karla, this is my gift to you, okay? Now take it and wear it."

I volunteered at the store for three years. The church's little thrift store worked a little differently from some others. You couldn't use money in the store. If you were on food stamps or Social Security, they would help you with food and clothing. If you had a job and needed office clothing or uniforms for you or your children, they would help you to get those items. They would let you work a few hours helping them out for the food or the clothing.

If you couldn't give a few hours to them, they would help you anyway. I wanted to help them because they had helped me. Some days I would walk up to the thrift store on my days off and work with the ladies at the thrift store all day. I helped them with whatever they needed me to do. I enjoyed just helping. I didn't feel like it was much to give, but I loved to give back to God.

Then the time came when I was losing my apartment. I realized that when the next rent time came, I couldn't make it. My light bill was $125. There was no way I could pay all my bills. I did my best and I prayed about it.

I went into the store and ran into a guy I had known for a few months. I didn't know "Joe" well. I had seen him in town. We struck up a conversation and I was telling him about what I was going through, losing my apartment. I also told him that a few months ago I had moved out of the women's shelter. I showed him where my place was in the projects. He was surprised. He told me I had to get out of there because it wasn't safe. I knew it wasn't a good place to live, but it was all I had. It was all I could afford.

Joe said he was looking for a roommate and we could work out how I could pay the rent. I made a deal that I would do all the housework for my part of the rent and buy the food. I didn't want to move-in with anyone, but it was that or my daughter and I would be on the streets. I didn't feel I had any other choice. He told me there would be no strings attached. I didn't want to be homeless again with my daughter. Still, the decision was a tough one for me.

I had made a promise to God not to move in with a man unless he was my husband. I broke my promise. I prayed to God for his forgiveness. I was so full of guilt for breaking my promise to God. Yet I felt I had no choice. Where would I go?

He helped me move in. I had my bedroom, and my daughter had

a bedroom of her own. I had gotten a new job that I could work and be home with her after I got off work. Then I would take her to school with me when I went to my classes.

It was time for me to do my taxes. I got back a lot of money that year. It was a little over $4,000. I put that money in the bank. Six months after I moved in with Joe, he started making moves on me. He threatened to put me, and my daughter, out on the streets if I didn't sleep with him. He was using his psychology on me. He had bragged that he went to college and got a degree in psychology. He used everything he had on me. He tried to make me believe he could read my mind. The abuse had started.

He told me that he was my hero. He felt that he had saved me by getting me out of the bad neighborhood. And he felt that he had saved my daughter, too. When he offered to let us move in, I'd had a bad feeling about him. I just didn't listen to the voices in my head. I didn't trust myself. I let my fear of being alone on the streets cloud my judgment. It has taken me a lot of time to trust that feeling that says, "he's not the right one." But right then, I was still too timid, too afraid.

Eventually, I gave in and started a relationship with him. It was a relationship I didn't want at all. I didn't love the man. In fact, I started hating him. I grew to resent him. I couldn't even take a shower every day without him getting in the shower with me. He made me feel so dirty. Then his abuse really got worse.

He would call me in a condescending voice and tell me what I needed to cook him for dinner. He would even tell me how to cook it. The mental abuse and the physical abuse began. He began to yell at me more and more often.

We had only been together for a few months and he wanted me to marry him. He kept asking me to marry him. I told him no. I explained that I wasn't ready to marry. I told him I had too much unfinished business with my daughter's father. In reality, that was just an excuse not to marry him. I was feeling trapped again. I had gotten out of the frying pan and into the fire. That's what I would tell myself.

I knew I was in another abusive relationship. The question was how was I going to get out of this one? I started reflecting on my life. I prayed about this. I felt guilty for breaking my word to God about never moving in with another man and sleeping with him before marriage. I repented every day I spent with that man.

Joe was so abusive. I despised him. Then he started trying to put a wedge between me and my daughter. He would punish her for silly things like not calling him "Sir." She would have to do all the dishes. If I told her that she didn't have to do that, he would jump all over me. He was so controlling.

The house had no air-conditioners. Florida is really hot. Doing chores during the heat of the day was very difficult. He knew about the tax money that I had in the bank. It was my money for the things that my daughter and I needed. It was my money, period.

He stopped working at his job. He just up and quit. He had a conflict with his district manager. She called him a liar. In fact, he had lied to her and told her that he had done something that he had failed to do. I was with him at his job when he threw a temper tantrum. He yelled at her just like he yelled at me. He told her that she needed to be at home, bare foot and having babies. Then he walked out and quit his job. For six months I supported him.

Well, one Saturday, he went off with his friends and he left me and my daughter at home. We were cleaning the house and the landlord came by and demanded the rent money. I didn't know that he hadn't been paying the bills. The man said he needed the money today or we would be out in three days. I didn't know anything about the laws. I got out my checkbook and wrote him a check. I didn't feel I had much of a choice. My paychecks were little, and I needed them for food and other expenses. That had been our original deal.

When Joe got home, I let him have it. Where was his money going? He grabbed me by the throat and choked me. He asked me how I could speak to him in such a manner. I told him I wanted to know where his money was going. I thought he should have the money to pay the rent.

He told me he was helping his friend Scott with some of his bills. He told me that he knew he could get my tax money. He did just that. He wouldn't work.

I wound up paying the rest of the bills until finally, my money was all gone. After all my money was gone, he got a job as the manager of a store. He would take my paychecks if I didn't cash them and turn them over to him. He would hit me until I would give him my money, or he would grab my arm and twist it till it would almost snap. I would fall to the floor crying. He knew where to hit me so that the bruises wouldn't show.

I found out that he had taken a belt to my daughter. He left stripes on her butt. I was livid with him. When Joe came home, I jumped him and ask him why he had hit my daughter. I grabbed a belt and started hitting him with it. I knew it wasn't right. In that moment, I had become a batterer. I hit him with the belt and told him that if he ever touched my daughter again, I would call the police. I told him I would not stand for him abusing my daughter. He took the belt away from me and he whipped me with it.

The hardest part of this event was the realization that I had become what he was. I was no better than him. I was so ashamed. Not only had I become an abuser, I had also put my life in danger as well is my daughter's life. I told him that I was saving money for me to move out. I had had enough.

He tried the honeymoon stuff. He bought flowers and gifts for my daughter and me. It didn't work. I knew that if I gave in, he would be right back to yelling and hitting. I had been in the relationship with him for three years. I could not take it anymore. I quit school.

He called my work repeatedly, trying to get me fired. I quit my job. I was still going to church and praying for God to help me. I went to the church altar and poured my out heart and soul. I prayed for God to forgive me. I felt I was paying for breaking my word. And I felt like my daughter was also paying for my sins.

I was so full of shame. I could not even tell my best friend about the hell I was going through. I prayed at the church altar asking for God's forgiveness and asking Him not to let my daughter hate me for putting her through the hell of moving in with this man. I felt like I had slipped deeper into hell. The despair I felt was so complete. I hated what I was doing. I cried myself to sleep for days. I prayed for God to help me again. I had created this mess. I had chosen this hell. I needed God's help to get me out.

I still can't forgive myself for the pain that I caused my daughter. It hurts me to this very day. I didn't have anywhere to go. I felt like I couldn't let us be homeless again. But I also felt like a whore, selling myself. God, how could I do this to us?

I cried over this. I prayed. I was most distressed when I thought about my daughter. I could take anything that the man did to me, but my daughter shouldn't have to pay the price. How could I have fallen so deep into despair? I had learned to keep secrets a long time ago. I kept so many things hidden. I couldn't even tell my best friend. I was ashamed. All that I could do is cry out to God for his help and mercy. I didn't feel that I deserved the help, but my daughter did. I tell this now to show others that it's easy to get back into an abusive relationship after you have left one. It's easy to fall back down that rabbit hole, and it may be worse with the next man.

I want all abused women or men to know that getting out of abusive relationships leaves you vulnerable. You could be open to getting into another bad relationship. There were several things that led to me getting back into an abusive relationship. I didn't have the skills or the support that I needed to help me. I didn't know who to trust. I didn't really know how to recognize an abusive personality, and abusers hide it so well. You are in before you realize it.

I take full accountability for all of my actions and the choices that I made. Everyone who comes out of an abusive relationship needs to find counseling. People who have been in an abusive situation need counseling as bad as an alcoholic needs Alcoholics Anonymous. We need help to understand why we stay in abuse, why we choose the people we choose.

I didn't tell my best friend about the relationship I was in with Joe. I couldn't admit how stupid I was by moving in with him. I felt as if I didn't have choices. I had no family to fall back on. I didn't feel like I could move in with my friend because she was very judgmental. Some of the things that she said to me cut me to the bone. Her words hurt so bad.

I couldn't stand up to her. When I tried, she would say things that were verbally abusive. She would say, "You're so sensitive." She didn't seem to have compassion. She was more like a mother to me than a friend. Some of my other friends would ask me why I stayed friends with her when she was so mean to me. I guess I accepted her verbal abuse because it was familiar. My own mother and I interacted in much the same way. My own mother put me down. But, like my mother, my friend had another side of her that could be just like an angel. She was two-sided.

I kept so many things hidden. I was good at keeping things hidden. After all, I had hidden family secrets my whole life. I had been through so much. I felt alone in my life, having to hide such darkness. I didn't think I'd deserved to be treated well. I felt as though I was judged by others. This feeling kept me in a cell of despair.

I knew that I had made mistakes. But I felt judged when my friend Vicki pointed out my mistakes. Her words could be cruel. She seemed self-righteous. I didn't need someone putting my face in the mud for what I had done. I couldn't ask for help from her. I knew she would feel it was a shame for me to move in with another abusive man. I didn't feel that she had the compassion that I needed. I knew she just couldn't understand what I was going through in my life.

Sometimes even Christians act in an unkind manner. Some Christians are self-righteous. It isn't a good thing to shame a person who's going through abuse. My friend didn't understand this kind of life at all. It was completely foreign to her.

In ways that I didn't understand, abuse was familiar to me. Sometimes I wondered if I allowed myself to be abused because it was all that I had never known. Life had taught me so many toxic things. I had learned very early in life that no one cared if a child was being abused.

I've learned toxic things. I learned to keep dark secrets. I learned about living in the dark closet of shame. I had experienced toxic parents. They enabled the darkness of taboo secrets like childhood sexual abuse. Family systems like this enabled the ugliness to live on. We all lied. We lived in denial. We didn't speak about what we all knew was going on within our family.

Children who are raised this way learn that abuse is okay. Many times, no one would stand up for them or help them in any way.

The seeds are sown for destruction. As a child from this kind of family grows older, they often breathe life into a new cycle of abuse.

Where is our accountability as people? Why do we mind our own business? When we put our heads in the sand, we enable the abuse to go on. Even court systems make excuses for perpetrators. I've known of people trying to get justice for their sexually abused child, only to be told that the perpetrator was mentally challenged and didn't know right from wrong. Where is the justice in that?

As a society, we need to make the guilty pay for what they've done to their spouse or their child. We shouldn't send a message that it's okay to be abused. We need to stand up and fight for those who cannot defend themselves. We need to hold ourselves accountable, too. We have to help, or at least try. We may not stamp out abuse, but we can change laws. And there definitely needs to be more laws to help protect the abused.

Someone told me a few years ago that things were different a long time ago, that women were considered a man's property. Men beat their wives, and no one interfered, because they felt the wife was their property. That was never a right way to think. A wife isn't something that you own. A person isn't something that you own.

I am telling everyone what I think about how the abuse cycle keeps getting passed on from mother to daughter or from father to son. Here is a question:

Mother, what are you teaching your daughter by staying with the man that hits you or is sexually abusing your daughter? How could you know about it and do nothing?

I could ask a similar question of a man who hits his wife. What are you teaching your son? Are you teaching him that love is about hitting?

If you stay with a man who beats or abuses your daughter, you are in denial. You may try to make excuses. You may say to yourself that it's only oral sex, if that's all it is. Or it's only touching inappropriately, as if that was some sort of lesser sin.

You may try to ignore it. You may tell others to just get over it. Forget it. It's part of the past. You may convince yourself that there's no real damage. That's where you are wrong. It does do damage. This is all part of the thinking that enables the cycle to continue.

Is living in that nice house worth all the abuse that's going on? Maybe you are trapped just like I was. There is always a way out. You have to find it.

Abusive relationships are not real love. They certainly aren't worth dying for.

As I write this, I am 48 years old. My mother chose to stay with my abusive father until he died. I know these are strong words, but it's the truth. And I was abused by my mother. I don't mean to disrespect my dad or my mother by speaking about the ways I was abused by them. They were both damaged people. But these were the roots of my toxic abuse, the roots of my life. I am breaking out of those toxic beliefs. I am healing.

I believe that people are better equipped for dealing with someone's house that's on fire than they are equipped to help someone out of an abusive relationship. If that isn't the case, then why is there still so much abuse in the darkness?

In my family, I was taught to keep taboo subjects in the dark. I was told not to report it when someone hits you. People don't understand, and don't know, how to help someone who keeps the abuse a secret. If you suspect that someone has been beaten, or sexually abused, encourage that person to open up to you. Don't be in denial or hide your head in the sand. Be a friend today to someone who needs you. That person may open up to you.

Denial is a dangerous thing. People stay trapped in a lie that will kill them or someone else. Denial is the biggest lie we tell ourselves.

People have to face the truth. Otherwise, they will never be able to move on with their lives and to deal with the pain of abuse. It's not easy dealing with emotional pain. We usually can't do it on our own. I suggest, if you are dealing with the pain of abuse, that you get counseling. Abuse is hard to talk about, but we have to try.

Speaking as a survivor of abuse, I hope this book will help. Overnight, we won't be able to change the world. I get that. But one compassionate friend can start. I hope that this book will help someone. Maybe a good friend will give it to someone they think it might help. Maybe this book will break the ice. I don't know. I hope so.

All abused people need friends. It is my sincere hope that my words can help someone avoid just a little of the pain that I have had to suffer. If a person was battered and couldn't speak about it, my hope is that this book could help them leave and break the chain that holds them. I know that if I can break the cycle of abuse, they can, too. But they need help.

After so many years of keeping secrets and telling lies to myself and to others, I want to be honest, to speak up more, to speak out. I want to go to churches and domestic violence shelters and speak to those who have lived in abuse or currently are in abusive situations. I want to help others the way I was helped.

Know that if you are in an abusive relationship, that you are not alone. God is speaking to me and God is telling me to say to you,

"You are not alone. He has seen you through your darkest night. He has loved you all your life."

God says, "Don't cry yourself to sleep anymore. You feel hopeless and full of shame. You are not alone, my child, for I am here. I have loved you for all your life. I will carry you. You are not weak. I will dry your every tear and heal the scars of your heart. You are not alone my child."

God carried me through all of my life's storms. I know that God is not finished with me yet. I walk in the healing and peace of God. God has counted my every tear, just as He counts yours. He is holding the bottle of tears in his hands. God is with you in the darkness. God loves you and wants the best for you. He wants healing and love for you. Never forget that God loves you and has never forgotten you. God really loves you.

- SIXTEEN -

Facing Him in Court

It was December of 2002 when I went to my mailbox and received a letter from the child support office. It was a letter that I had been expecting for almost a year. I read the letter. My heart began to race. I felt so many feelings at once. Here it was in print. Roy and I would be facing off in court for child-support.

I dreaded facing him in court, but at the same time I wanted to get all of it over with. I prayed as I kept reading the letter. I asked God to let me be strong when we went to court. I asked Him to let me do what I have to do for the sake of my daughter. I even got a friend to coach me about what to say in front of the judge. I was very intimidated about going before the judge. I knew I would have to face Roy and I didn't want to show my old weakness. I didn't want him to know that I was afraid of him. I'm sure that that's what he expected of me. I just had to stand up to him once and for all. But the thing that was uppermost in my mind, was that I had to live as an example for my daughter.

There would be several court dates. When the first date came it was scheduled for early morning. I walked up the courthouse stairs. I can remember it vividly. I placed my hand on the rail and took each step slowly as I prayed to God. I told God that I knew it wasn't His will for me to fear Roy. I knew it wasn't God's will for us to be fearful. I told Him I would face Roy with strength and calmness. I repeated the mantra, "I will not fear Roy."

"In Jesus name, I will give you my fear. I will face him, and I believe that you will walk with me, God. I believe it with all my heart. God, you are my strength. I ask that you give me the right words to say to the judge. God, please don't let my words shake with fear as I speak."

As I took that last step I said, "In Jesus' name I will not fear. I will face this with strength. Amen."

I opened the door and walked into the lobby. I had to look for the courtroom that I was supposed to be in. I felt all my fear leave my body. I was so calm looking for the judge's courtroom. I found it. As I was walking, I saw Roy. He spoke to me as I passed. He said, "Good morning, Shorty."

That was the nickname that he had always called me. I said with complete confidence, "Good morning, Roy."

He mumbled, "It didn't have to go this far. We could've worked this out."

I just smiled and kept on walking. Roy tried to rattle me with his mean looks. I took a deep breath. I glanced over as Roy settled on the bench next to mine. I could see that he was clenching his jaws. I knew by this that he was mad. I prayed again to God, "I will not fear him, in Jesus' name."

I got up and walked over to the water fountain.

I lady walked up to me and asked me if I was Karla. She said my last name as well. I told her, "Yes, I am."

She was holding a thick file. I could see Roy's name on the tab. She said she was representing me in court. She said she was with the Internal Revenue Service. I was surprised. I told her I didn't have any money to pay her to represent me. I didn't know why she was going to court with me. She told me not to worry about it.

She was there on my behalf and it wouldn't cost me anything. So, I told her okay and she sat beside me on the bench. Roy was still seated on the bench beside us.

We sat there waiting for the court officer to come out of the door and call my name. I thought of Roy and his temper. I thought about the times he had come after me. I remembered all the talks we had about his ex-wives and how he hated them and about all the things they had done wrong. He always had such contempt and resentment for his son's mother. He had always assured me that no woman would get child-support from him. He had always told me, "Not a damn dime."

I know it wasn't really my place to say anything about his previous relationships. But this time I was fighting for my daughter and it was my place to say a little.

The first time someone came after Roy for child-support was when the state of Georgia came after him. It was 1996 and we were living in Florida. We had been living in the big house that he was trying to buy. He had been paying $600 a month to purchase the home, which he was buying from a doctor. He wouldn't put my name on the house payments (documents).

That summer we went to the mall for something and there was a lady asking if we wanted a store credit card. I asked Roy if I should fill out the form. He said to fill it out, but he didn't think we would get a card. At the time, my daughter was about three years old. Roy did get the store credit card. I think that filling out the information to get Roy the store credit card was what got him caught for the past child-support he owed to his ex-wife.

When he received the card in the mail he went shopping. He bought a big TV that cost about $3,000. He bought DVD players and all kinds of toys. He maxed out that credit card. He couldn't make the credit card payments. Somehow, he managed to get about five more credit cards. He was living big in his eyes. He could buy more beer and stay drunk all he wanted.

In 1996 I had gone to court with Roy when the state of Georgia came after him for child-support. I took all of the bills to court. I also took our daughter. When we went into the courtroom, the judge asked why the minor child was in the courtroom. I stood up and said I was representing my daughter. I wanted it on record that Roy was supporting me and our daughter. The judge wasn't happy, but I submitted the bills Roy had to pay. The judge ruled that Roy's child-support payments would be seven dollars a week for his son. I felt sick after I realized what I had done. Roy always had a way of making everything about him and not about his children.

Now it was 2002 and I had received a letter from the state to enforce child-support on Roy. I knew he would be mad at me for breaking my promise not to come after him for child-support. Sometimes you have to break a promise. It's more important to do what's right for your child.

Of course, Roy's parenting patterns told me he wouldn't pay child support. It was pretty sad, but it was what it was. I wanted to do what was best for my daughter. I wanted to do it right and by the law and I wanted to do what was morally right.

I called a male friend, Andy, that had I met riding the city bus. He had helped me learn how to ride the city bus -- what to do, which bus went where, and where to get on and off. He taught me how to get where I needed to go, and he helped me to learn how to calculate the time that the bus would arrive so that I could always be on time. I didn't even know how to get the bus to stop for me when I first started riding it. My friend Andy showed me how to make the bus stop.

So, when I first got the letter from the state, I called Andy. He met me at a sandwich shop, and I showed it to him. He told me what the letter meant. Because of my dyslexia I couldn't read it and understand what the entire letter meant. We sat eating a sandwich and talked about me facing Roy in court. He asked me what questions I had about going to court. I told him I didn't have any self-confidence about standing tall and facing Roy. Maybe a lot of people would have thought it was not a big deal. But to me it was a huge deal because I had never done this before. I was so insecure. I had no idea what to expect.

Andy told me that the judge would probably call so many people in at a time. I would be called and so would Roy. Andy told me to only speak when the judge asked a question. He advised me to give a yes or no answer or short facts. He said judges do not want long, drawn out answers. I took mental notes. Andy gave me a book that had words in it that lawyers would use in court. It was a book of words that helped people study for the bar exam. I told my friend Andy that I felt like I sounded stupid. I felt like I would sound like a Kentucky girl going into court sounding stupid and looking stupid. I just had no self-confidence at that time in my life.

Andy told me that the judge would take into account the amount of money that Roy made. The judge would determine the child-support based on a standard. He may be ordered to pay monthly, or he could be ordered to pay weekly or bi-weekly. I explained to Andy that Roy worked for money that would be paid under the table. This meant that people were paying Roy cash for his work, so he didn't have to report it and the business didn't have to pay taxes on him. I was afraid there would be no record of his pay. I knew Roy would lie. I felt he would say he didn't have a job. I knew better.

I told Andy I wanted to do right by my daughter. I couldn't afford an attorney. Legal aid didn't think I qualified for their help. Andy told me he would get back to me about the questions on proving what Roy made in salary for a week.

Andy researched it and told me I could testify in court if I saw him getting paid within 30 days of going to court. I went to see Roy on Friday. I knew he got paid at lunchtime, so I made sure to go then to let him see his daughter.

Roy used to spend so much of his time working on racecars with his buddies. I had finally realized that he just didn't want to be married or be a father. What I thought was love really wasn't. He wanted someone to control and to clean house and cook for him. He didn't want the responsibility of a family.

We didn't get a copy of our daughter's birth certificate until she went to school in 1999. The one that we had from the hospital the doctor had not even signed.

It was December of 2002. It was court date for us. I had a friend to do my hair. I was so scared. I put my hand on the railing to walk up the courthouse steps. I paused for a minute and I asked God to give me strength and the courage not to be afraid, then I said, "Amen."

As I stepped on each step I said, "God, I will not be afraid today. I will face him with courage and strength."

I stopped shaking inside. I sat down at the tables that were near the courtroom. Roy said, "Well, looks like you started this."

The court officer came out of the doors and called out names. He said he only wanted those he called to come into the courtroom. There were about half a dozen couples in the courtroom. I took a seat. I tried to see Roy's face. I wanted to see what kind of mood he was in.

Roy was sitting on the other side of the room clenching his jaws.

I could see his cheek muscles moving. I knew he wasn't happy with me for what I was doing. This court date was to establish child-support.

The judge wanted us in her chambers. The court officer and the stenographer came in to record what was being said. Roy walked in with his lawyer. He seemed smug. They both sat across from me. I didn't have a lawyer.

In walked the judge. The court officer said, "All rise," and we were all sworn in. The judge called both of our names and began to talk. She said "This was a marriage of 20 years…"

I spoke up, "No ma'am. We only lived together."

She said, "Oh, the state of Florida does not recognize common-law marriage." Common-law marriage is when people live together for a long period of time as if they were married. Many states consider such relationships legal after a certain number of years. She noted the correction.

She asked if there was a DNA test to show who the father was. Roy spoke out. He said, "I have no doubt judge. She's mine."

I handed her the DNA results. She read them to Roy, "It's 99.9% that the child, Victoria, is your daughter."

She asked, "Who has custody of the minor child?"

I told her, "I do."

She asked me if I had a job. I told her where I worked. She asked me how much I made. She also asked if I had medical insurance on my daughter. I told her I didn't have medical insurance because the job that I had didn't carry medical insurance. All I had was Medicaid for my daughter. It was the best I could do. I told her I was going to school to get my high school diploma. She said that was good.

After that she asked Roy, "Why aren't you paying her child support?" She told him that he owed my daughter $13,000 and the state of Florida $1,000. He told her that he only made $6.30 an hour. I knew it was a lie. I had proof. I didn't say anything at that time.

She looked at him and said, "Roy, I will only accept two reasons why you can't pay her child-support. Those reasons are if you are dead or you are in a coma."

I was surprised. I thought, "Wow, she's not playing his game."

I asked the judge if she could order him every other year to pay for our daughter's school uniforms and school supplies. I told her that uniforms were expensive. She said she didn't think that was too much to ask. He was ordered to pay child-support of $50 a week or he could pay it by the month.

Well, three months went by and he didn't pay a dime. We had to go back to court. I was wondering if we would get the same lady judge. And even though it was three months later, we did get the same lady judge.

I wondered if she remembered us. I was full of nerves again. I hated facing him in court. I could tell he wasn't happy. Still, I couldn't let him intimidate me. I wasn't backing out. I knew I couldn't back out now because the state had made me sign a paper saying that I would file for child-support.

This time was a little like the first time going to court. Again, I sat there listening for our names as other people were called. I was thinking that the judge would be asking us the same kinds of questions.

I saw the first case go in front of her. I looked at how they both were dressed. One mother filing for child-support was there. The father of the child was wearing gold chains and brand-new everything as if he were ready to go clubbing. He had on brand name shoes, jeans, and a brand name shirt. The judge started off with her questions.

It was interesting to note that some of the people in court who were ordered to pay child-support were women.

The first question that the judge always seemed to ask was, "Why aren't you paying child support?" In most cases it was the same pitiful answer. People told her they didn't have a job. Some said they could find a job. The judge commented as she had before, "The only two reasons I will accept for you not paying child support is if you are in a coma or you are dead."

She asked the question about their assets. She asked them if they owned a car. Some of them would say yes and some would say no. I could see where her questions were going. She was establishing if the man was lying about his assets. I was amazed that so many people tried to con the judge.

I may have felt a little calmer this time. The judge had told me that I would have to come back in a few months. I wasn't looking forward to it. But I would deal with it and be strong. The other thing that I would be was prepared.

I got a friend to take Victoria and me to Roy's shop where he worked. Victoria asked me to take a picture of her and her dad at the shop. I took a picture of them with my cell phone. He gave her $20 to get her a toy or something. Then we went home.

I was thinking about when we would have to go back to court. I had forgotten that I had a newspaper clipping of Roy and his boss standing in front of the race car showing the machine shop's logo on the car's hood in the background. The newspaper where he worked wrote a piece on what a great machinist Roy was. It really was a good piece that the newspaper had written up on him. I had saved it for Victoria. Roy was, after all, her dad.

That newspaper clipping would come back to bite him in the butt. This is a southern saying. It is something we say when something you do comes back to haunt you or get you in trouble. It's kind of like karma. Karma can be a boomerang that can hit you right in the face.

Roy wasn't paying the child support he was ordered to, so he got a summons for contempt of court. I looked up the word. It wasn't good on his part. The judge could fine him and put him in jail.

I got all the papers I that I needed for court, including the newspaper write-up on Roy. I was trying to think how he would try to lie his way out of this one. I knew he would. He showed the judge such disrespect. He didn't like her because she was a woman judge. He didn't like women to be in control of him. He just wasn't happy, and I knew it.

I knew I had to be there in court at eight in the morning. Since I had to be there on time, I couldn't ride the city bus for fear that I would be late. I was going back to court. I wore my same light blue suit and the simple pearls. I had a friend to do my hair and makeup again. You could tell I wasn't one of these women that went to the hair stylist every day. My suit looked like a second-hand suit. Nothing I wore was brand-new. It all came from a secondhand shop for used clothing. I had asked a friend to drive me. She waited in the parking lot.

I walked up the stairs outside of the courthouse. Once again, I stopped at the first step and said a prayer. I said, "Heavenly Father, I know it is not your will for me to fear seeing Roy again in court. Please give me the strength I need and the right words to say to the judge so that I don't sound like a hillbilly or sound stupid. Thank you, Lord. Amen."

I sat on the bench outside the courtroom. Roy was looking angry and smug. He said to me, "Why so worried, Karla? It's just the money game you all play. Damn bitches." He then came over and patted me on the head.

I got up and went to the water machine. I sensed he was getting upset. I didn't want to have to deal with him or speak to him. He was trying to scare me. He was dressed in a black polo shirt and brand-new boots. I remember thinking how sad it was that he could buy himself brand new boots but couldn't buy his child any shoes.

The judge called the first case. She was going in alphabetical order. I didn't know if they would go with my last name which started with an "M" at the time or Roy's last name which started with an "S."

The first guy went before the judge. The woman and the man were sworn in and the judge read the charges. Everyone was in court for the same thing, which was contempt of court for nonpayment of child support.

The young man dressed in all new clothes: jeans, shoes, and gold jewelry. It seemed like all the people that owed child support were dressed nice and were wearing new clothes. The ones that were needing child-support were dressed like me. Their clothes didn't seem new but were clean and pressed. I would guess that they were wearing the best they had.

The judge didn't look happy with the first guy. She asked him if he owned any assets.

"No judge," he said.

Then she asked him, "Do you own a car?"

"No judge," he said.

"Do you own a house?"

"No judge," he said.

I wondered why she was asking all of this.

She asked, "Do you have a job?"

"No. I can't find one."

"Where do you live?" she asked.

"With my mom and dad."

I was starting to see a pattern with the questions she asked people.

She asked him, "If you sold all of your clothes, how much money could you get?"

I thought, "Wow, she really isn't playing with these deadbeat parents." It didn't matter if the deadbeat parents were women or men. It didn't look good for any of them.

As luck would have it, Roy and I were last. We were sworn in. I was thinking that this wasn't going to be good for Roy.

"What do you do for a living?" she asked Roy.

"I am a master machinist and I build engines."

Of course, he didn't tell her that he built race engines. He was afraid to tell her that, because that would mean he would have to pay more child-support.

Roy smiled at me from across the courtroom. I didn't respond back to him. I thought, "Boy he thinks he's going to play the judge." She didn't seem too happy with his answers.

The judge asked him how much money he made an hour. He told her that he made $6.30 an hour. She had seen this on the paper-work. She asked, "Is that a typo?"

He responded, "No, judge, that's right."

I raised my hand to speak.

The judge said, "Miss, I will get to you in a minute."

So, I nodded my head okay. I put my hand down.

She asked him, "How much do you have in your wallet?"

He reached to pull out his wallet.

She said, "No, I want you to tell me how much you have in your wallet. Everyone knows how much they have in their wallet."

She looked at me. "Ms. Karla, do you know how much money you have in your wallet?"

I said, "Yes judge, I do." I started to tell her, but she stopped me.

She said, "No, Ms. Karla, I am not asking you your amount. Only him."

"Ten dollars," Roy said with a smug look on his face.

I was wondering where she was going with her questions, because her questions to Roy were a little different. She did also ask him some of the same questions she asked the others. She asked him if he owned a car. He told her no.

I was thinking, "Here we go again with the games."

She asked him if he owned the house.

"No, Judge," he answered.

"Do you have a TV?" she asked.

"Yes, Judge."

She said, "Okay, Roy, if you sold your TV what could you get for it?"

"Oh, probably about $50," he answered.

I shook my head. He was lying. I raised my hand.

"Miss. I will get to you," she said.

"Roy, why haven't you paid your child-support?" she asked.

He said, "Umm, work has been slow."

Finally, she turned to me. She said, "Now Ms. Karla, you seem to disagree with Roy about a few things."

"Yes ma'am," I said.

She asked, "Do you have knowledge of him making more than $6.30 an hour?"

"Yes, I have proof that he makes more than that. He's a master machinist. Roy builds race engines for the machine shop. Every week he brings home $500 and half of what the machine shop makes with him building race engines. I have the proof."

She said, "Okay, where is your proof?"

I pulled out the newspaper clipping of him that was written. He had a uniform on with the logo of the machine shop. I told her that the newspaper article was written six months ago, but he still worked there. I told her that he was lying to her about his pay. I gave the clipping to the bailiff. The judge looked at the clipping.

She asked me, "Karla, have you seen him in the last month getting paid this money? Do you have proof that he still works there?"

I told her that I had taken our daughter to see him and his boss. I told her that Roy and our daughter walked into his boss's office and he paid Roy in cash. He counted out $500 to Roy. Then Roy gave our daughter $20.

She asked if I had any proof that this had happened within the last 30 days. I told her my cell phone had the picture of Victoria and her dad wearing the same uniform. The photograph had the date on it. The judge asked to see my cell phone picture.

She asked Roy again if he got paid on the day I was talking about. He told her no, that I was lying.

I shook my head no. She asked me if I had any other proof that he was lying.

I told her, "Yes, he's lying about his TV. I have the store receipts to prove his TV is worth more than he said. He has two TVs. One of them cost him $3,000 which he bought a year ago. Here is the store receipt."

I wasn't sure whether she believed me or him.

She looked at Roy. "Are you getting paid cash?" She asked him.

He said, "No, I get paid by check."

I shook my head. He was lying.

She asked Roy to take out his wallet and count out the amount of money that was in it. He didn't want to do it. I think he was afraid he would get busted for lying, but he took out his wallet. He counted his money. There was $110 there.

The judge said, "Well, it looks like you have lied to me. Now tell me why you don't have the money to pay child-support for your daughter?"

Roy said nothing.

"Roy, I want you to give $100 to the bailiff." I could see that Roy didn't like what she said.

He said "But, Judge, that's all the money I have."

She said, "No, Sir. You have $10."

Then she said, "I find you in contempt of court for not paying child support. Karla has proven that you can afford to pay for child-support. I believe her. I believe that you were lying. I believe you're getting paid cash to hide what you really make. You still owe her 13 grand. You will pay it or go to jail. You must pay her three months of the child-support that you owe her in the next two weeks. If you don't, you will go to jail. The only reasons I will accept for you not paying child support is if you are dead or in a coma. I think you're still alive and you don't seem to be in a coma."

Wow. This judge didn't play. I could see Roy's angry glaring. I was getting scared. I started to shake.

She called him a deadbeat parent. Roy was really mad at me. The judge said the case was done. I just stood there shaking. I didn't want to walk out of court near him.

"Is there something more Ms. Karla?" I couldn't speak.

"Are you afraid?" I nodded my head. She called to deputies to walk me to my the car.

Two weeks went by and the deadline was only a week away. I got $1,800 in payment for child-support.

I found another job before I went to court the next time. I kept working. The job I got was another hotel job. It didn't pay the best, but I was getting what I and my daughter needed. I had taken a shift that allowed me to be home when my daughter arrived home.

Roy didn't want to see his daughter. This really hurt her. I would call him and beg him to see her. Roy just had a lack of interest in his daughter's life. How do you explain this to a child?

I gently would tell her the truth. I knew she had every right to love her father and to have a relationship with him that wasn't tainted by my feelings. I knew that trying to get him to stay in her life would be hard. I knew this because he had other children and he was not involved in their lives. He had walked away from them and hadn't paid child-support for them. I had no reason to believe that my daughter would be treated any different.

- SEVENTEEN -

God Showing Me My Strength

The chapters of my life have been written. I feel God has shown me so much about myself; some of it good, some of it bad. There were things in my character that needed strengthening. He showed me many things that I lack. I am not talking about worldly things. He showed me my immaturity and my faults. All of the things He showed me were to shape me into the woman that I am now. His plan for my life was unfolding.

There were many times I got off the path and made detours. There were different errors that I had to repeat to grasp the lessons from them. He was teaching me. It wasn't easy at the time. He has shown me that He gives us all choices in life and everything we do is a choice. Sometimes our choices can take our life. He has shown me that when I stopped growing emotionally, I was stalled in life. I couldn't move on. I became bitter. Depending on where you are in your life when the growth stops, you may not feel the bitterness that begins deep inside. My love for Roy slowly eroded. He wouldn't let our love grow into what it could've been. I don't believe it was God's plan for him and me to be together forever.

I went through so much in order for God to shape me into who I am now. The scars of life and the abuse will last a lifetime. It's the scars that people don't see that concern me. Emotional, mental and verbal abuse leaves scars deep inside. Roy had no empathy for my feelings.

I was devalued when I was a child. The behavior that was modeled for me by my parents was incorrect. I was taught that women were solely dependent on a man. My value as a human being, let alone as a child, was zero. Many women were taught, as my mother and grandmother were taught, to depend on a man. Your value depended on a man. My value was even less than zero because of the stigma of my depression and my undiagnosed dyslexia.

My twin sister and I were born prematurely, at eight months. I don't know if that caused my dyslexia, but premature birth or low birth weight are risk factors, as well as exposure during pregnancy to nicotine, drugs, alcohol or infection. My mother taught me as if I were mentally slow. I guess I did appear slow as a child. I didn't learn as fast as my older sister, who was an over achiever in everything she did. My mother was trying to teach me to write my name before I went into school. I was left-handed. She didn't like me being left-handed and called me retarded. I didn't even know what the word meant. I accepted it and did my best to please my parents.

I developed coping mechanisms. I felt that the way my parents treated me was the way they felt about me. Their actions spoke loudly. Not being able to learn to read, I was labeled. The label followed me through most of my life. It was part of the reason for the low self-esteem, the seeking of approval, and being susceptible to someone like Roy, who showered me with gifts and attention.

I remember stories my grandmother told me about her being the "taboo woman" because of her being divorced. Back in her days, which were the 1950s, a woman had kids and stayed married. Even if the husband was abusive, they stayed.

My grandmother broke the rules. She divorced her drunken, abusive husband. He was also abusive to her daughter who was my mother. My grandmother was told that she could not receive her ex-husband's money for child-support. Her mother, my great-grandmother, told her, "Well, if you are not married to him, you are not taking his money."

This made it hard on my grandmother raising a daughter alone. This was the attitude they had back then. It was a bad one. My grandmother even brought another shame on herself. She remarried and had a baby by another man. That was looked down on by my great-grandmother. These kinds of actions just weren't done by a good girl. My grandmother was damned if she did and damned if she didn't. She couldn't win with her mother. What was passed down from my grandmother to my mother was to stay in an abusive marriage no matter what is going on. My mother did stay with my dad until he passed away over 19 years ago.

My mother taught me that when I marry, I should stay with my husband even if he was a controller and was abusive to me or my children. That's so wrong. Many families taught this. I believe it is wrong for so many reasons. My mother was taught to keep quiet about any abuse going on with her marriage and her children. When you keep this abuse quiet, you condone it. The abuse thrives by keeping it quiet and in the family. I was told when I tried to tell about the abuse I was suffering, "Oh, that is not talked about."

The secret was always known by the whole family. We didn't approve of it. We just didn't talk about what we knew about it. In fact, they have the false belief that by doing nothing it would go away. Many families believe this, and it is so not true.

Pretending it is not happening won't make the problem go away. Children who are forced to keep the deadly secret and to have no one to go to for comfort, help, or even compassion, become depressed adults. Those who have mental illness of any kind are almost an outcast to the family. They are treated as if they are defective.

My mother was treated that way by family members. Her mother-in-law always treated my sister and me, and my mother, as outcasts because we were the product of my mother's mental illness. I felt like my family was ashamed of us because of my mother's mental illness. We didn't speak about my mother's mental illness. We were taught not to. Where was the love and compassion for my family? These are the things I saw growing up. I hated what I saw. The knowledge I got from what I saw growing up made me sick. It truly affected my mental and emotional health. Where is our compassion for our fellow men or women or children?

I believe God would want us not to judge people with mental illness. I also know that mental illness is hard to cope with, for the person with mental illness and the family members dealing with the person. Bipolar is hard to deal with. As a child, dealing with my mother's mental illness, I felt I was shunned. We kept my mother's mental illness a secret as we were taught to do. Sometimes, parents teach life lessons without saying a word. I grew up learning to keep so many secrets. That was toxic.

I believe people must really start talking about the taboo subjects like abuse of women and men and children. Every generation that is taught some of the old ways of hiding abuse just keeps them going. Then there are some people that dare to step out of the toxic, accepted beliefs that have been taught to us. I have stepped out of the pattern of abuse. I have learned from it, and I want to try to make a difference. I am determined to change my life story. Writing about what I've learned has helped make me stronger. In my life, I have learned it is best to be a very open book. I want to make a difference in this world by writing and speaking out about the abuse and inhumane ways we treat each other and our children most of all.

Abusive people can't or won't see and recognize the damage they do to the spirit of a child. Adults who choose to abuse people are wrong. God has shown me my strength as well as my faults. He taught me to accept myself and others. I see the human factor. Some people just don't get what abuse does to people's lives. Abuse affects the person by shaping what and who they are becoming.

My father was ashamed of my mother's mental illness and we all tried to hide it from the outside world. I have such compassion for my mother, because of all she went through as an abused child. The actions and attitudes that we repeated from my mother's past were repeated because we had learned those lessons by observation and subtle instruction about mental illness and about abuse – keep it quiet, keep it a secret inside the family circle, and accept the status quo.

At the same time, God showed me that my mom didn't know how to be a mother. Her mother treated her so differently than she treated her sister. Why? Who knows? I guess that's one of those old secrets the family kept that may never be revealed.

God has shown me about my life. He has shown me the life roots that were passed down to me through the generations. God showed me that the non-value I was shown by my parents is part of what caused me to be ashamed and caused me to feel that I was a burden to my family. I left home so young.

These are some of the dark seeds I carried. Like my mother, I had no one to turn to for help. When I did try to talk to someone, I was often blamed because of her shame. So I learned at a very young age to keep the secrets in the dark. I didn't speak about the taboo subjects like abuse of any kind. The abuse would live on. But now, I lift that veil of darkness. I speak out to those who are broken from abuse. Let's give compassion, help, and advice. Let's tell others where and how to get help.

God has shown me my strength, and that it's not easy to have strength when I see so much sadness. God has shown me so many things. Parts of my life I have total peace over. When I meet people now, I don't know a stranger. I don't cower. Maybe this book will teach others to speak to anyone in need of help. There are many kinds of abuse. I have learned to accept myself. You don't get respect from others until you respect yourself.

For years I have never felt accepted by my parents or friends. At the age of 49 years old, I have finally learned that only I possess the gift God has given me. In Him I have my value and self acceptance. This is a priceless gift. I have to help myself heal as well as asking God to provide my healing needs.

No one but God can make my scars heal. I believe that knowledge is power. Now, it is placed in your hands. You have to take the steps to help and heal. Where would you start today? One small step in your life will carry you to a better journey. You can't heal alone. You need God's help. If you can afford counseling, seek counseling. Life doesn't come with an instruction manual. Children don't come with an instruction manual. You do the best you can with what life gives you. I felt that life dealt me a handful of Joker cards. I've learned how to turn the Joker cards into aces. Sometimes I even keep the Joker cards and laugh at myself. You have to live your life honestly and then peace will come to you. I know with God's help and perhaps some counseling you will make it. I did!

- EIGHTEEN -

What Effect Does Abuse Have on Children?

Abuse has many lingering effects, depending on the severity of the abuse. The child could have been hit. Very often, if a woman is abused by her husband or boyfriend, her child is abused, too. In my case, living with someone who would act like a drill sergeant to my child was difficult for me to watch. Rules were made daily on what she could and could not do. My child was a wreck dealing with my abuser. She tried to please him. The wind could blow and it would set him off on a tangent. He would yell all day at both of us. She and I were walking on eggshells. That left its mark on me. What did it do to my child?

What we learn as a child in terms of discipline is, many times, carried over into adulthood. I want to stress that this is not a certainty. Just because the child's parent is emotionally or physically abusive does not mean that the child will grow up being abusive to their own children. Sometimes they become just the opposite because they are aware and acknowledge how the abuse made them feel, and they don't want to put their own child through the same thing. But sometimes we have to learn the right way to discipline, just as we have to learn other skills. Discipline should include compassion and love.

The rules Roy came up with were insane. He tried to overpower my authority as her mother. He presented himself as if he had a role that mattered more in her life, than I did. My daughter became depressed and withdrawn from him. She wouldn't deal with him. She wouldn't even talk to him unless she had to. But when we went to parent-teacher meetings, he would put on the charm. He would be kind to my daughter and me in public. Later, he would brag about how he could manipulate everyone. He would brag that he could talk his way out of anything. He believed his own lies of how great he was. Substance abuse, angry outbursts, feeling helpless, and having a less than adequate self-esteem can all be an outgrowth of abuse. Had Roy been an abused child? I don't know, but I suspect he was.

There have been studies showing the things that children have learned when subjected to abuse. There are negatives from observing, as well as experiencing, trauma. Some children will survive and become great, loving parents and do not implement these negative traits. The converse is also true; abused children frequently can either become abusive parents, or be the opposite, too lenient. They fail to instill boundaries and allow the child to have the rule of the home. We know childhood traumas can and will impact their lives in many different ways. We should never minimize the impacts of abuse. Identifying the impact on the children's lives is difficult. As a survivor of domestic violence, I had to seek and implement changes in my life. My choices affected my daughter. I wanted better for her and myself.

I know abuse does affect children in many ways. Children raised in an abusive home may have more illnesses because their immune system is stressed by the effects of abuse. I am not a doctor nor a nurse, but I have made observations in my life about living in abuse with my daughter. I noticed that my daughter got sick easier, and I believe it was because of the stress in our lives.

Symptoms of childhood abuse may show up in life at different times. I wanted a peaceful life for myself and my daughter. I possessed a passion and a willingness to get better and to not be defensive. Looking at one's own issues is imperative. By telling my life story I will break down the walls of abuse one brick at a time. On the other side is freedom from the ugliness of a painful past.

Healing can bring a better life to myself and my daughter. I have a purpose to help all that seek help in understanding the effects of abuse on the family. I can live on and the abuse can be stopped.

I took for granted that the abuse I was living in only affected me. But I started to see, while living in the women's shelter, the effects of the abuse on my daughter, and other children. As I watched the children play, I was seeing the effects of the abuse on the boys. They were aggressive. They were at play and some of the mothers would give their sons, in a blink, excuses regarding why the boys were so violent in their play with the girls.

When I asked the mothers, "Don't you think your son was affected by seeing you get hit?" Their response was, "Naa, he just went to his room and watched TV."

I am disclosing in my stories about my relationships and the role I played in them. I made bad choices. I had to get to my roots of where my thoughts and feelings came from. Why had I made the choices I had made in my life? Why did I think like I did? I had to understand myself. I had to discover what real life was supposed to be like. My understanding of love was different than the love I was living. I thought I knew what love was. As an abuse victim I needed to focus on the pains of my past in order to heal. I am blatantly honest about my shortcomings. My shortcomings created loneliness and despair.

Now, for the first time in my life, I know what love is. The tragic reality is that any time a mother is abused by her partner, the children are also affected in overt and subtle ways. What hurts the mother, hurts the children. When a mother is abused, the children may feel guilty that they cannot protect her, or they may think that they are the cause of the strife. They may themselves be abused or neglected while the mother attempts to deal with her own trauma.

The rate of child abuse is higher in families where the mother has been abused in her past or childhood. I've learned this from my own past childhood abuse and observation. Children can feel confusion, fear, shame, and guilt, and any combination of these at different times. They may think that they cause the problem. Children who see their mothers getting beaten develop emotional problems. Boys who see their fathers beat their mothers are more likely to be abusive in their relationships. Boys who see their father hitting their mother may learn to abuse their wives or girl-friends in the same ways. Some, fortunately, will vow to never abuse anyone the way their father did.

Abuse does affect the children. Children may have emotional problems, be withdrawn or shy. They may cry a lot. Children may have a fear of adults or have problems with friendships. Children may suffer from depression. They may be sick a lot and miss school. Children may use violence for solving problems. Children may run away, think of suicide, or have problems with the law. Children who are stressed can show it in different ways, including difficulty in sleeping. They may sleep a lot more, have a bedwetting problem, become stressed over-achievers, or their school grades may drop. They may develop behavior problems, withdrawal, have stomachaches, or get in fights. Problems could be manifest as headaches and/or diarrhea. They may get involved with drinking or drugs to escape the abuse. Children who grow up in violent homes have much higher risk of becoming drug abusers or being involved in later abusive relationships either as a batter-er or a victim.

Children do not have to be abused themselves in order to be impacted by violence in the home. Domestic violence must be treated for what it is – a crime. We must fight the societal values that reinforce the stereotypes that encourage men to act aggressively, such as: men using violence to solve problems; men thinking that women are weak and should be submissive; that women should accept male dominance as the norm.

Children must be taught nonviolent conflict resolution at an early age. In a home with domestic violence, the terror, instability, and confusion replace the love, comfort, and nurturing children need.

Abused children live in constant fear of physical harm from the person who is supposed to care for and protect them. They may also feel guilt for loving the abuser. Domestic violence is our problem, and we must take steps to change the laws and be more helpful to abused women, children, and men as well.

When violence occurs, call 911. Show the police any injuries. Keep medical records and take pictures of injuries. Document the abuse. Report abuse even if the batterer says it didn't happen. Get it on record. Don't be afraid to report it. It could save your life.

Never be confrontational. Don't yell in his face, "I'm calling the cops." That may get you killed. Abuse won't go away just because he says, "I won't hit you anymore, I promise."

Abusers must get counseling if they really want to stop hitting you or your children. It's a long process. Most abusers will be good for a while and then con you into believing they've stopped being a batterer. After the "honeymoon" period they are likely to go back to their old ways and it often gets worse.

- NINETEEN -

The Path to Self-Forgiveness

God has taken my hand going down many paths of life. He's taken my hand in this current path which is self-forgiveness.

God has taught me so many things about myself. I know that forgiving Karla is very important. It's not the easiest thing for an abuse victim to have self-love. Toxic messages play inside my head. These were messages that my parents taught me from such a young age. What is a toxic message? It is telling yourself things like, "A child is to be seen and not heard." The messages the child hears are: "Keep your mouth shut." "You don't know anything." "Your opinion doesn't count." "You are not important." "Your voice shall not be heard." "Your pain doesn't matter."

If your parents have told you these types of things, how did that make you feel inside? Did it hurt? Did you just accept what was said without a thought? As for me, I accepted the hurtful words. Many people simply don't think before they say such toxic, hurtful words. The hurt gets worse when your parents' actions add to your pain. Parents thoughtlessly say things like, "Shut up," when you tell them something so painful and they don't believe you or they tell you that you lied for attention.

My parents taught me self-hate and shame when they blamed me for what the perpetrator did. Blaming the victim for being raped is toxic. It's wrong. When I told my grandmother that I had been raped, she asked me, "Well, honey, what kind of underwear were you wearing?"

It was as if she believed that I asked for it, that I somehow caused it. I know this is a coping mechanism that she developed. Denial means, "I don't have to deal with the muddy feeling of empathy for my granddaughter." "I don't have to face the perpetrator with the accusation."

This coping method happens all the time because we as children are taught to deny our feelings of pain. We are taught, "Don't be a crybaby."

I know you've heard that one. All the feelings I was taught as a child were toxic and I've had to deal with my emotions about these things later in life. This is a parenting trait of many dysfunctional families. I am fighting my way out of this toxic mess.

As I write this, I am 46 years old. Have you ever put it together why so many from my generation are hooked on booze or prescription drugs? Maybe the pain of being told all their life that they didn't matter caused this to take root. It goes so much deeper than what I've spoken. My parents treated me as if I was a burden. I was told, "You're a social illiterate, but honey, I love you even though you're stupid." They said they loved me even though, or because, I was flawed. I believed them. I couldn't learn self-love while being denigrated. But God loves us for us.

When you are sitting by yourself, looking at yourself, what do you see? If you start saying things like "Well, I've got a pretty nose but a big butt." This is negative self-talk. Just say, "I love you for all that you are." Can you do that?

I know I pick myself apart. Self-love starts when you love yourself no matter what. My parents put me down by saying things like, "My daughter's pretty but she's stupid as a box of rocks." My parents taught me to be critical and judge myself harshly. This teaches us to see the worst, not only in ourselves, but in others. This is judging and we should judge others as we would want to be judged. Now I am being shown by God to love myself and forgive myself. God accepts us for who we are, even with all our faults.

Karla Reeves

- TWENTY -

Finding My Best Friend

In 2004, I went to the public library. I went on a website that would help you find classmates. I posted that I had been looking for a friend of mine named Donald.

Donald had been a little red-haired boy with an accent. He had moved into my town back when I was in high school. He was a year and a half older than me and a year higher than me in school. We were involved in National Junior Reserve Officer Training Corps. I really noticed the boy with red hair and blue eyes. My class in N.J.R.O.T.C. was going on a field trip for a week. We were getting on the chartered bus, and I took my seat on the bus near the front. This red-haired young man placed his hand on my seat. Our eyes met and I smiled at him. I looked down. I was a little shy. There was just something about him. I didn't know what it was.

Our class went swimming. We were doing drills. We were all in a line and were supposed to pretend we were on the ship. We were to cross our arms and jump off the ship into the pool. Our teacher asked our class who could swim. We made two lines at the swimming pool. One line was for the ones that could swim. The other line was for the ones that could not swim. I was in the line that could swim. I really couldn't swim, but I thought I could. I didn't know at the time that doggie paddle didn't really count as swimming. There were two lifeguards in the pool. I didn't know how deep the pool was, but I knew it was deep.

We watched the sailors do the exercise. They would jump into the water and stay afloat. This sailor showed us that if we couldn't swim, that there were things we could do to keep us afloat. We could take off our jeans and fill them with air. We tied a knot at the pants leg cuffs to make our jeans or pants fill up with air and float. They showed us how to make our pants into a float to keep us from drowning. I thought it was really neat.

We got on the platform. We called my teacher "Chief." He instructed us what to do. Before any of our class did the swimming exercise, they had someone show us what to do.

I was next in line to do the swimming drill. I took my place.

He told me, "Cross your arms over your chest and jump in feet first."

I stepped up to do as I was told. He said, "You need to stay afloat for five minutes."

I crossed my arms and jumped in feet first like we were shown. I went deep down. I opened my eyes thinking, "Oh Lord, I can't swim. I thought I could."

I don't know how deep I went into the pool, but it seemed like a long time before I started coming back up. I was struggling. I was inhaling and gasping for air. I was struggling to swim, but I was drowning.

I hadn't made it back to the surface of the water. I felt big strong arms grab me around my waist. Someone was pulling me to the surface. I opened up my eyes, coughing water.

He said, "Hold on to me. Don't fight me. I will take you to the side of the pool."

I held on for dear life. He looked at me and said, "You can't swim, can you?"

I whispered, "No."

He asked me, "You know you could have drowned?"

He lifted me up to the side of the pool. When I got out, Chief wasn't happy with me.

"Miss Karla."

I said, "Yes, Sir."

He said in a stern voice, "You could have drowned."

"Yes, Sir," I said. "I thought doggie paddling was swimming."

"No, it's not," he told me. "Well, you can't finish this exercise. You have to go down to the shallow end of the pool with the other babies that can't swim."

This is when I really got to talk to Donald. I walked down to the other end of the pool. Everyone asked me what had happened. They saw me nearly drown. I told them what had happened to me. I sat down and Donald and my other classmates started talking.

Donald and I could talk about any subject, even when we didn't always agree. It was okay. He was the one that I could share my deepest secrets with, and I knew he wouldn't ever break the bond of our friendship. I told Donald some of my darkest secrets. He was the only person that didn't judge me or walk away from our friendship.

Donald and I talked. We talked about everything. I had dated his best friend. Donald and I would sit in the gym and we talked about everything. We solved the world's problems. I would notice if Donald was absent from school. I would miss him dearly. When he was back in school the next day, I would see him from down the hallway of the vocational building, and I'd be calling his name as I ran down the hallway.

"Donald, Donald, Donald!"

There was a time or two that I almost knocked him down as I ran to him down the hallway. I would hug him as if I was his long-lost love.

We had something very special in our friendship. I didn't know what it was. It was a feeling that was new to me. Others would ask if Donald and I were dating. I would tell them no. Some of my friends saw something in my friendship with Donald that I couldn't see, or perhaps didn't know what it was called. Maybe it was love, even then.

No matter what the problem was, Donald was always someone that I could turn to and not be judged. He would speak to me lovingly. Donald was unlike any friend I had ever had. He never betrayed me in anything I ever told him. He was what a real friend was supposed to be. I think that was what made me love him. Donald and I, at times, seemed to be loners in high school.

Getting back to the website, I had posted my e-mail address and a note that I was looking for my best friend Donald. On the website I put my e-mail and after I got his first e-mail message, I sent him my phone number.

My heart began to race as I looked at my phone and the number was from my home state. It must be Donald.

"Hello," I said.

"Hello back," he said. His voice took me back to our time in high school. He graduated before I did, and I had lost track of him. I dropped out of school after he graduated. I had moved to Texas after that. The last time I saw him was in the early 1980s.

Donald and I both held our breaths as we began to ask questions.

He asked, "Are you married?"

I told him, "No, I never married."

"Didn't you marry Roy?" Donald knew Roy.

I told him, "Roy and I lived together, and we had a daughter together."

"Why didn't you and Roy get married?"

"Roy never wanted to marry me."

Donald began to tell me slowly of his feelings for me. He told me, "Roy was a coward for not marrying you, because you had a baby together."

I began to ask him questions about his life and his family. I found out we were both single. Donald didn't have any children.

Over the coming weeks and months, I began really opening my heart to Donald, telling him about the hardships I had as a single mother and the problems that I was having getting child support.

I told him about the man I was currently living with. I began telling Donald about the abuse I was going through. It was really hard talking about the physical abuse and telling him about how hateful and abusive the man was to me and my daughter.

On one phone call, before we hung up, Donald said, "Karla, I love you."

This blew me away. I swallowed my pride and told Donald something I had never told him. Back in high school, I had feelings for him. I swore before God that if I ever found my best friend, Donald, I would confess to him that I had loved him back then. I felt the feelings of love for Donald back in high school days, but I was so backward and inexperienced, I didn't know what the feelings were. Now, as an older woman, I could tell him that the feelings were of love.

The feelings for Donald had never died after all those years of being apart. Donald was always in my heart and in my thoughts. I only had our class picture of him and me in our class uniforms. I had kept it so that occasionally, I could see his face. I knew deep in my heart my feelings of love for Donald would never die.

When I thought back to those high school years, I thought, "If I ever find my best friend and he tells me he's happily married and has kids I would gladly settle for just being his best friend again."

I wanted to be a part of his life, even just as a friend, I would never interfere with his life if he had a wife and children. The situation was very different once I understood that we both were unmarried.

On one phone call, out of the blue, he asked me, "Why don't you just come back to Kentucky with your daughter?"

I told him, "I can't leave with my daughter. I am currently battling Roy for child-support."

Deep down, I really wanted to move back to my home state, but I didn't have the money to relocate with my daughter.

Donald said, "I want to ask you something. Would you move back to your home state if I came and got you?"

"Yes," I said. I never hesitated.

He told me that he was getting time off from work soon. He advised me to pack my bags. This was very scary for me. I was living with a man that abused me and my daughter. I had to leave him. I needed to get out. Donald was offering me a means to escape.

- TWENTY-ONE -

The Plan to Leave

There were so many things I had to think about. I was leaving this abusive man. I had to talk to Donald. I had to come up with a plan for how to leave. I needed to get my daughter and myself out safely. Donald and I were talking about making a safety plan for us to leave.

I did a lot of praying about how to leave Joe. There was one evening that Joe would be working late at the store. I began talking to my daughter. I told her that I had been talking to my best friend from high school about her and me leaving. I told her that Donald was willing to help us leave Joe and get back to my home state. I told Victoria that Donald and I were making a safety plan for us to move back. I told her that on the day we would be leaving, I would send her to school and then Donald and I would come to get her. She wanted to help me pack.

That night, she and I packed boxes and put them on the back porch where Joe wouldn't look or see them. It was October 18. The deadline was coming up soon. I told Donald that we could leave on Wednesday. I told Donald that would be the safest time.

Every Wednesday, Joe would have to be at the store at 5:00AM and he couldn't leave until after 5:00PM. The store always got a shipment of things and all the staff had to be there to unload the truck. No one could leave until the truck was unloaded. I knew that I had a window of time from 5:00AM to noon that no one could leave the store, no matter what. That was my safety window to get myself and my daughter out. At 4:00AM I got up and fixed Joe his breakfast. I tried to make things as normal as I could. I turned my phone ringer off. I saw missed calls from Donald. I couldn't get caught talking to Donald that morning.

Things might fly apart if Joe found out I was planning to leave him. God only knows what would happen to us. I couldn't take that chance. I didn't want Joe to find out what was really going on. Then, while cooking Joe's breakfast, I got a text message.

"I am in the parking lot of the grocery store." This message was from Donald. The grocery store was nearby. Taking a deep breath, I tried to stay calm. I would be getting Joe out of the door soon. I would be getting my daughter off to school soon. I had to pretend that my daughter was going to school as usual. You may ask why I made things look as normal as possible. Joe's best friends lived next door. I couldn't take the chance of one of them calling Joe to let him know about us leaving. I just couldn't take that chance.

By 8:00AM, all his friends from next door would be gone to work. Joe's friend Sam would be driving past us when we were waiting for my daughter's bus. Things had to look normal. I was looking at my watch waiting for the time to pass. I would get my stuff packed and moved out. I was trying to keep myself calm.

I got Joe off to work. He told me he would see me after 6:00PM. It would be a long day. I told him I had put Gatorade for him in his lunch box. I told him that tonight he would have a surprise for dinner. The surprise was he'd come home to an empty house. I looked out the window. I watched his car lights leaving the driveway and pull into the street.

I got out my phone. I called Donald to apologize for not calling him sooner. He told me he was standing by. He was waiting in the parking lot. He was waiting until it was safe for him to come to the townhouse.

I told him, "Just a little longer."

I was getting my daughter up for school. I told him to wait until I called him after 8:00AM. By then the coast would be clear. I told him that I loved him. I was packing more stuff. I was getting my important papers ready to go. He said a prayer for me over the phone.

I felt calmness come over me. I knew things would be all right. I got my daughter up for school. She wanted to help me pack, but I told her that things would have to look like she was going to school. I didn't know if I could trust Sam not to call Joe and tell him we were leaving. I told her she would be safe at school. Donald and I would be there to get her before lunchtime. I had fixed her breakfast. We walked out the door to the street for her to catch the bus.

My phone rang. It was Donald wanting an update. I talked to him. I was speaking to him when Sam drove by us waving good morning.

"Good morning," I said. I waved back, smiling.

Sam's roommate was gone. Now I had to get my daughter to school.

Donald said, "Tell Victoria to look at the red truck right behind her bus."

There was Donald waving at her from a rental truck.

She waved back at Donald.

I hugged her and told her that it would all be over soon. I would be there soon to get her.

She kissed me and said, "I love you, Mommy."

I told her, "Things will be okay. I love you, too."

She got on the bus. Donald was still driving his red truck right behind the school bus. I was waving at him. It was all that I could do not to run and get into his truck. I was so excited to see him. I told him to meet me at the store.

I walked to the store and there he was. My best friend was waiting for me. I went back in time again. I was running down the hallways as a teenager. I was calling out his name, "Donald, Donald, Donald!"

I fell into his arms. I could feel his heart racing as fast as my heart. I was holding him so tightly. I didn't want to let him go ever again. I looked up at him. We both were a little older in years. Our eyes and our feelings, however, were the same. He looked the same. I looked into his blue eyes and it took me back in time to our youth. When we met all those years ago, I just couldn't get over his smile.

"Karla, I love you," he told me. He gently kissed me on the lips.

"I love you too, Donald," I hugged him again.

"Karla, I told you I would come for you and your daughter. I will keep you safe. I won't ever let you down."

As we both realized the reality we were facing, he said, "Let's get this thing done, Hun. Let's get you and your daughter out of this hell!"

I got into the truck telling Donald, "Everyone is gone from next door."

Then, I was surprised and disappointed to see Sam's other room-mate's car in the driveway.

"Oh shoot," I said. "Jackie's home. He's Sam's other roommate."

Donald said, "Well, it's do or die. If she calls Joe, we're going to deal with him, but we've got to get packed. Are you okay to leave? It's now or never?"

I looked at my watch. I told him, "In one hour we are leaving no matter what. Help me keep a watch out for Joe's car."

Inside the house, I ran up the stairs. I was nervous and I lost my footing. I fell down the stairs. Donald ran to catch me.

He said, "Take a deep breath, Karla. We can do this. It will be okay." He held me for a moment. Luckily, I wasn't hurt; only my pride was hurt.

We both packed and moved things into the truck. For the fiftieth time I looked nervously at my watch. "It's time, let's go."

He asked me, "Do you have your purse?"

I was almost in a panic. "We must go with or without my purse. I can replace everything in it."

I jumped in the truck. I walked out of the townhouse for the last time. I didn't look back. It may seem odd, but I did this to strengthen myself. I wasn't going to look back. I had to look forward to tomorrow.

"Where is her school?" Donald asked. I told him how to get to her school.

I went into the school to get my daughter. I told them I didn't have my ID with me. Of course, this held me up in trying to get my daughter withdrawn from school. I went back out to the truck.

Donald asked, "What's taking so long?"

"I need my purse."

He looked in the truck while I went back in. I was praying that Donald would find my purse. The counselor was out to lunch, so I had to wait until 1:00 o'clock until she got back.

I was delighted when I saw Donald come in carrying my purse.

"Thanks, Honey. You found it!" I said. I explained to him why I had to wait.

"It's going to be okay." He hugged me again, "Take a deep breath."

The counselor came back in. They called us to the counselor's office. I told her I had a family emergency. I told her I was withdrawing Victoria from the school. I told them we were moving to her grandmother's and would stay in Kentucky.

She asked, "Is this her father?"

Before I could say anything, Donald spoke up and said, "Yes, I am her dad." Then he shook the counselor's hand. I had not expected him to say that. I just smiled at him. He took my hand and squeezed it gently as if to say once again, "It will be okay."

They had us fill out forms and told us to wait back in the main hallway. They would send for Victoria. As we sat down, we saw a line of kids coming back from lunch. I heard a little giggle.

"Hi, Mommy." It was my daughter coming back from lunch.

I mouthed the words, "We are here to get you." She waved back. She followed the rest of her class.

The lady in the office said we could take her with us and put her in the Kentucky school. They would send us her school records. The hallways went quiet as the next bell rang. I heard footsteps and a backpack with wheels coming down the hall. I was praying it was her, and it was. As soon as she saw us, she started running to us. I told her to go with Donald to the truck. I had only one more paper to fill out.

She grasped Donald hand, "You must be Mom's best friend."

He picked her up as he hugged her. Donald said, "She looks just like you, Karla. She's so beautiful." I just smiled. I knew she would be safe. She was already asking him about our two cats. I could hear him telling her that they were both in the truck. "We weren't going to leave your babies."

I gave the lady in the office the other piece of paper. I was more relaxed. The lady commented that Victoria looked like her father. I just smiled and told her, "She's a daddy's girl." I got finished and I walked out the door. It felt like a big rock fell off my shoulders.

Donald told my daughter what we were going to do. We pulled out of the school driveway. I knew that we had a day and a half drive ahead of us.

I was so frazzled and yet I felt relaxed for the first time in a long while. Donald had given my daughter a little pocket game to keep her occupied during the long drive. Victoria asked Donald many questions. They both talked back and forth. He told her about our plans. He would rent a place for us and pay my bills until I found a job. He would help in any way he could.

We drove for six hours. He asked if we were getting hungry. We all were getting hungry by now.

As I was getting out of the truck, Donald looked at my cats to see if they needed food and water. He handed me a bag with food and a pan of water for them and I gave it to them.

He said, "They look like they are doing well." He hugged me.

I told him, "Thank you."

He looked at me and asked, "Thank me? For what? I love you. This is what you do." We shared our first real kiss in the parking lot.

"I love you, Karla Jean. Let's eat." We went and got food. My heart was still racing. I was thinking of so many things. We drove for the rest of the night and Donald and I spoke about the plans we have.

We drove into the next morning. We watched the sun come up. I felt safe for the first time in my life. My daughter was waking up. We were near the Kentucky state line. I began to tell my daughter about the state I had come from.

Donald asked, "Why don't we stretch our legs and go to the bathroom?"

I walked to the ladies' room. Victoria had run ahead of me. I didn't see her. I went into the bathroom calling her name. I could hear her, but I couldn't find her.

"Mom, Mom." Just then she came into the room where I was. "Mom, you are in the wrong bathroom. This is the men's bathroom." We both giggled.

I told her, "Looks like your mama needs to learn how to read, don't you think?"

"No, Mom. You are tired. You've been up all night." We both got back to the truck and Victoria climbed in. I hugged Donald again. We were both tired. He had driven all night. He took my hand and said, "Let's get something to drink from the soft drink machines."

I said, "Sure." As we walked, Donald dropped my hand. I was still talking about something. Suddenly I realized he was no longer walking with me. He was behind me doing something. I turned around. He was kneeling on one knee. He pulled out a white box. He took my hand.

"Karla Jean, will you marry me and be my wife? I love you and I want make a life with you."

I was stunned.

"Karla, I got your daughter's permission to marry you." Victoria was looking out the truck window and smiling.

"Yes," I told him, "Yes, I will be your wife. I love you, too." The ring was too small, so we kissed to seal the promise of marriage.

- TWENTY-TWO

Is My Marriage Blessed?

We drove to his mother's house. We were all tired and needed sleep. No one was up. My daughter went to sleep in the extra bedroom. Donald and I sat up talking for a few minutes, just unwinding from all that had happened in the past few days. We went to Donald's room, which was off to the back of his mother's house. Even though I hadn't meant to, I fell asleep in his arms. We didn't want to sleep together until we were married. I told him I had made and broken one promise to God, and I wouldn't break another one.

He respected that and said, "No problem."

He told me he wanted our wedding to be special and be pure. I know that's a little old fashioned for this day and age, but it's how we both felt. I slept until about 2:00PM that day. When I got up, Donald was already up. He knocked on the bedroom door.
"Let's get out and see your hometown."

I got a shower and got ready to leave. It was a very warm, 75-degree day. It was October 21, 2005. I had a peaceful feeling that day. I asked Donald if the weather was a bit warm for October here in Kentucky.

"Yes, it is," he said. So I put on one of the summer dresses I had packed. When I had packed it, I had thought that I wouldn't need it until next summer. But I already had to get it out.

We went driving around the town in which I had been raised. The little town had really changed since the 1980s, when I had left. I couldn't believe it. I was really back home where I belonged. I had prayed for years to get to move back to my hometown. Thirty-some years had gone by since I had left. I had really missed it.

We drove down the road I used to live on when I was younger. It was amazing to see how things had changed. We drove past my parent's old home. The place where I had grown up seemed much smaller than I remembered. My little hometown had grown and changed.

I felt good. I remembered all the prayers I had sent up to be home again. God had taught me a few things about prayers. He taught me to pray and believe with all your heart and have the faith of a child. He taught me to let go of the prayer and let God do the rest. The second part of the lesson was that sometimes the answer of the prayer may be "yes," and sometimes it would be "no," and sometimes, it would be "later."

The next thing I learned was that in God's time you will get the answer. Sometimes, the answer may be very different than what you want. The fourth part of the lesson was God does give you the deepest desires of your heart and soul. God has to guide you down the path for you to receive the joy of your soul.

Something else I had prayed for many years was for God to send me a man who would love me for who I was and not want to change me. I had learned many of life's lessons with the men that had crossed my path, but I had to do some growing and changing for me to cherish the love that God would send me.

Many years ago, a woman I knew who had the gift of "seeing" had predicted that I would meet Donald. She told me about Donald, but I couldn't see clearly like she could. She told me that the man I would marry was in my past waiting for me. She said that I had met him in my youth. She also told me of the great love he had for me and he would treasure our love. I had always remembered her words, that one day God would send a man to love me. All that she had predicted was coming to pass.

Donald and I held hands as we went to get something to eat. We could hardly eat, we were laughing so hard. We were just having a great time.

Then he said, "Let's get married today!"

I looked at him and said, "It's a great day to get married. Let's go to the courthouse to get the marriage license."

I looked at the time and it was 3:30PM. We could just make it in time. I asked the ladies at the courthouse if someone could perform our marriage ceremony.

She told me, "Over at the office across the street."

We went across the street. There were two couples in front of us. They finally called us in and asked if we had a witness. We hadn't even thought of that and didn't have anyone with us.

The Preacher was reading the vows and I said, "I do."

He said, "Not yet." We both giggled. You could tell that I had never been married. We both said our vows. When it came to the part where Donald was supposed to place the ring on my finger; it didn't fit. It was too small. Donald was trying to push the ring on my finger, but it wasn't working.

The Pastor said to Donald, "Spit on her finger."

We all started laughing harder. I told him to stop, that it was hurting. I said that I had a ring in my purse. I had a silver ring with a three karat pink stone. It was my daughter's birthstone, and it fit perfectly. He placed that ring on my finger. We giggled all through our vows.

I looked at Donald and said, "May we both laugh throughout our marriage. May we both love and laugh always." Then the Preacher said that we were married and we could kiss. It was a day when two hearts bonded as one.

My hair was windblown. I wore no make-up. I had no pretty white wedding dress, just a simple blue summer dress with palm trees on it. But that was okay.

We were heading to the park where my father last worked before he passed away. I wanted to see the pear tree they planted in my dad's memory.

I kept asking, "God, is my marriage blessed?"

I heard someone say, "Rainbow."

I looked at Donald, "Did you say something"?

"No," he said.

I heard the word, "Rainbow" in my ear. I looked on my side of the road. I didn't see a rainbow. I heard the word louder, "RAINBOW, RAINBOW, RAINBOW!"

I said, "Oh, my God. There it is! Stop!"

Donald slammed on the brakes and pulled off the road. I jumped out of the truck. Right there in front of me was a full rainbow. Donald grabbed his camera and took pictures of the big, beautiful rainbow.

I asked him, "Have you ever seen a full rainbow in October"?

It was God telling me our wedding was blessed. I love rainbows. I told Donald about hearing the word rainbow. I just felt God's presence and it was just beautiful. We went to see the tree they planted in Dad's memory. We headed back to his mom's house.

The next week we got moved into our house. The first week we were married, Donald got medical insurance for my daughter and me. It was the first time in our lives we had real medical insurance instead of medical insurance from the state.

Before the week was up, I made a call I was dreading to make. I wanted Roy to hear from me that I had moved back to our hometown and gotten married. Three days after I had called him, I got a certified letter in the mail.

I was so glad that Donald was home from work. The letter was from Roy. He wanted me to have sole custody of our daughter. The next day I received another letter. Roy wanted Donald to adopt our daughter, but he demanded that Victoria keep his last name. I called Roy about the letters. Sure enough that's what he wanted. It was just crazy. Donald and I didn't have the money for him to adopt Victoria, so we left things as they were.

I had the child support case transferred to Kentucky. It went back and forth, going to court for contempt. He wouldn't pay child support; then, every six months, or whenever he felt like it, I would get a check for $2,700, a child support check.

Two years into our marriage, Roy moved back to Kentucky. I didn't know what he had on his mind. I was afraid he would fight me for custody. He was so unpredictable. He had left years ago because he wrote bad checks on his ex-wife's account. There had been warrants all over town for him. He had waited for the statute of limitations to be up. I felt he had chosen to come back to our hometown now, when no one could touch him, but I didn't know for sure what his reasons were for coming back. He and his family didn't always get along. His mother was getting up in age. I tried not to worry about him. I had to take one day at a time.

Then came the day when he called me and wanted to see our daughter. I didn't want him to see her, but I knew the law. He did, after all, have rights and I couldn't tell him no.

We told him to meet us at his mother's house. It was the 4th of July. Victoria didn't want to go with Roy. She wanted me to go with her. I told her I couldn't, and that she must go with him. He was her father.

Then she said, "No, Donald is my dad." She grabbed Donald and held on to him.

Donald told her she had to see Roy. We told her to take my cell phone and keep it on and call or text if she got scared, or if she needed us, and we would come get her. I was breaking into pieces over having to make her go.

Roy pulled up in his truck dressed up in leather jacket and wearing new boots. We all tried to be kind and civil. He said that they would go for an outing, maybe go shopping, and to see her grandmother. My daughter was trembling as she hugged me.

She whispered, "Mom, please. I don't want to go."

I told her, "You are his daughter, too, and you have to go with him." I told her to keep the phone on at all times, and to text if she wanted us to come and get her. I had to establish trust in Roy. I had to let him see his daughter. If I kept her from him, I could lose custody. He could take her from me. He had a right to see her as long as he wasn't hurting her, or beating her, or wasn't drunk. She hugged Donald and me. I went into another room and just broke down and cried. I didn't want to let her to see me cry and I didn't want her to go with Roy. I didn't know if he would bring her back. The thing was, custody of her wasn't settled. As her father, he had equal rights unless he abused her.

I just prayed as they left. Donald comforted me. He didn't like it, but he knew the same as I did, that Roy had rights. We both hoped and prayed Roy was trying to change and maybe become a better father.

We just didn't understand, why now? Why did he want to be a dad now? He hadn't wanted to be a parent to Victoria when we lived in the same state. We didn't know if it was all a show for his family, or what. I knew he didn't want to be a dad, the way he had treated Victoria and his two sons.

We both watched the time go so slowly by. Every time we heard a car driving up the road, we both kept looking out the window, waiting for him to come back. It was about 11:00PM when we heard a truck pulling in the driveway. We almost knocked each other down to see if it was Roy, then we both ran back to the couch to act like we weren't worried. The doorbell rang and I opened the door. I was calmer when I got the door opened.

My daughter hugged me as soon as she came in. Roy said he wanted to take Victoria again to a family cook-out. We said ok, but we still felt uneasy about him having her. We gave her my cell phone each time, until we could get her a cell phone with GPS on it. I knew it wouldn't keep her safe if Roy acted crazy and didn't bring her back, but we had to keep the faith and establish some kind of relationship for our daughter. Now that he seemed to want to be in her life, I welcomed it, for her. Still, in the back of my mind, I wondered why he wanted to be a father after all these years.

We were at Donald's mom's house and Roy came up. He had his son, Victoria's older half-brother. I was surprised to see his oldest son. I thought, well, maybe he's making an effort for his kids. I couldn't help but wonder how long this would last. They left and before too long, he brought Victoria back.

I had framed one of the pictures Victoria had drawn. It was a lily drawn in charcoal and watercolors. She had made me one, but this one was different. It was in color, and just beautiful. Roy, his brother, son, and his nieces were in the living room.

As a kind gesture, I gave Roy the picture. Roy's mood went from having a good visit to dark. I could see Roy's happy mood melt and drain down his face to pure anger as they left.

Donald's parents didn't understand why Roy's mood went from pleasure to anger. They, too, could see something happen. Then Donald said, "I think I know what happened. It was the picture that you gave Roy."

I asked, "What about the picture?"

He said, "What last name did Victoria use when she signed it?"

"Oh, Lord. She signed her name as 'Reeves,'" This was Donald's last name, not Roy's.

I didn't mean anything bad by giving the picture to him. It was only meant as a kind gesture from parent to parent. I was proud of her artwork. I remembered we had gotten a letter from school saying that she was writing her last name as Reeves, not her birth name. We had to tell Victoria to stop writing the wrong last name. Victoria only wanted to be part of our family in name. She wanted to belong to Donald, too.

Well, after that, Roy's visits stopped. He had called me after that day telling me that his daughter needed to tell him she was sorry for what she did.

I thought, "This is crazy. What does she need to apologize for?" I guess for the picture, but I wasn't going to make her tell him anything. She had just wanted to just be part of a real family. Before the call ended, I still extended the welcome to visit her any time. The phone went dead. He had hung up on me. We went back to the old game of him not paying child support.

He had only visited her six times before things changed. He even took her shopping and bragged about spending $300 on her. It felt like he was trying to impress someone by spending so much money on her, but I thought, "At least he's trying." But it didn't last. The calls stopped and so did the visits. Roy was reverting back into the man he was in the past. It all just seemed to end without a word of 'why' to her. It all seemed like a big game to him. But it was our lives.

There wasn't anything I could do but accept who he was and to try to keep the door open for him to see his daughter. No matter how I felt, Victoria had the right to love her birth father and have a relationship if she wanted it.

- TWENTY-THREE -

The Christmas Card from Dad

December 23, 2006. I went to the mailbox and Victoria had received a letter from her birth dad. I thought, "Oh, wow."

I didn't usually open my daughter's mail, but I did this time. I was worried about what it might contain, and I didn't want to subject Victoria to any more pain.

Inside the letter, I saw the card he had sent her. I guess I had a devastated look on my face.

Donald asked, "What's wrong?"

I told him, "He's sent her a Christmas card."

Donald said, "Oh, cool."

I said, "It's not cool at all."

He asked, "How bad can it be?"

I told him that Roy had sent her a ripped off envelope for a card and told him what it said.

"It can't be that bad."

I was almost in tears as I handed him the envelope.

"You can't make this stuff up," I said.

The card smelled of smoke. His letter told her that because he had sent her money, he would only have $3.00 to spend on food for the week because he had given her the last $20.00 he had. I knew it was a lie, designed to make me feel bad about the child support. I broke down in tears. Some would say it is the thought that counts. Words just couldn't describe how I felt about the "wonderful card." My husband was so upset that he posted a blog.

I felt that the thought behind the card was to hurt us. I was protective of my daughter. Victoria had been through a lot. It was a poor excuse for a card. I didn't understand how he could do that to his child. It really cut deep. I took a picture of the card, because you had to see it to believe it.

Donald's blog touched my heart:

"I'll never understand the person who hasn't a clue when it comes to their children. I've never had kids of my own, but I do have a wonderful step-daughter who is the light of my life, along with her mother, my wife.

"Divorce can tear kids apart emotionally because they just don't understand why it happens. Mom is Mom and Dad is Dad in their mind and there is no piece of paper, nor is there an excuse in their world that would change this fact.

"Why is it that some adults who are parents can be so cruel to the ones they helped create? Especially when their kids have done nothing to deserve the cruelty they are receiving?

"I know divorce can be ugly, especially when one parent tries to pit the child or children against the other parent.

"What about a parent that tries to keep the parental bond togeth-

er, only to have the other take it out on the child? This was a child who had done nothing to deserve this kind of treatment. Why do parents who pay child support use that as an excuse to hurt the child?"

Roy had been abusive to me. I didn't want him to be abusive to my child. When you have a child with an abusive man, his presence can continue in your life due to his parental rights.

I cried when I saw what my daughter's biological father sent her for Christmas. I can't describe the look in her eyes or the tone of her voice when she saw it. She handed it to me and told me to throw it away. She didn't want to see it again.

My husband and I had taken pity on him before the card was sent. We had offered him a one-time deal to help him because he was so far behind in child support. Donald talked to me about it.

He wanted me to talk to Roy about him sending us a big child support payment that we would cash and mail it back to him. This would have required trust on both of our parts.

When Donald and I talked about doing this, I didn't like it.

First off, it would be helping him when he didn't want to pay child support. I also didn't like it because it was a fraud. Donald had gotten soft and wanted to help Roy. I knew that Roy didn't want to do the right thing, no matter what it was. But Donald talked me into calling Roy to talk about this offer.

That conversation didn't go too well. Of course, Roy didn't want to do that. A week later he calls to ask if we could do it. I guess he had thought about it.

I told him, "That was a one-time offer, and you didn't take it the first time. So, no deal." He got mad at me and hung up.

Karla Reeves

- TWENTY-FOUR -

Mixed Feelings and the Adoption

It was February 2009. Donald and I were talking to Victoria. We asked her if she wanted Donald to adopt her. She wanted it. We told her we would get the process started.

We went to the lawyer's office, Attorney "Lucy." We told her that we wanted to file in court for Donald to adopt my daughter. She said we would have to get Victoria a lawyer "ad libitum." The lawyer would represent Victoria. She said they would contact Roy.

I gave her the two letters that Roy had sent. She laughed and said the judge wouldn't allow my daughter to keep his name. She thought that it was pretty arrogant of Roy to ask that of a judge. It was like a slap in the face.

She said, "Your daughter's name will be Reeves." She told us that it would probably take a month or so to get a court date. We wrote her the check, paying her $2,000, the full cost of the adoption. We asked her who would be a good lawyer for our daughter. We made an appointment with the lawyer and it went smoothly. I'll call him "Mr. Grant."

Mr. Grant said the case would be easily accomplished. He said he would contact the birth father. I gave Mr. Grant Roy's address and the two letters.

I said, "He just moved back to Kentucky a year ago." He asked us why we had waited like we did.

We told him we wanted to let our daughter settle in and to see if Roy would keep in contact with her. We had wanted him to be a part of her life.

He asked us how many times Roy has visited her after he moved back. He was surprised that it had only been six times.

I told him I thought his current girlfriend was trying to cause problems. When I would call her house to speak to Roy, she would get upset with me. She would say things like, "Why are you calling?" I tried to keep things open for my daughter's sake. I think the girlfriend was either insecure or jealous. It got so that she wouldn't let Roy take my calls. I just stopped asking him to visit his daughter. He wouldn't call her, and the last visit had gone badly. It was with all these things in mind that we decided to put an end to this. Roy's actions spoke volumes. It showed that he didn't want to be a part of her life. He wouldn't call, and I believe the reason was that he wanted out of the child support. It was time to close this chapter.

After I left Roy, he had proposed to me and told me to my face the only reason to marry me was to keep child support off his back. He was childish and selfish. He was who he was. I couldn't change him.

I did try to respect his girlfriend. She was married years ago. She went through the same thing with her ex. She had to raise her two children by herself with no child support. She seemed to understand what I was going through, and I really respect her for sometimes paying Roy's child support.

She told me on one of the times that I spoke to her, that she was paying his child support. I told her I was grateful for it. I left it at that. I didn't want to say more, but I know Roy was using her to pay his child support obligations, just as he had used me.

We talked to both of the lawyers a week before we went to court to see if Roy had responded to the adoption papers. Victoria's lawyer said Roy had come in a few days after he got the paperwork. He said he was too happy to sign his rights away so he could get out of paying child support.

The day was fast approaching to go to court. In a few days, the adoption would be finished.

April 25, 2009, we had to be in court at 8:00AM, We let my daughter stay home from school on the day of the adoption. We would take her to school after we finished things up.

Victoria was 15 years old. I felt so many things about that day. Part of me wanted Roy to show up and fight for her. I hoped for any sign that would show me that Roy loved her. I kept looking at my cell phone to see the time.

In walks my daughter's lawyer. The lawyer wanted a few minutes to talk to her. A few minutes later, my lawyer walked in. She gave us the okay sign. Things were about to start. Since they went by the person's last name, we would probably be in court a while.

Some people were at court for non-payment of child support. At different times, the door would open, and I would look to see if it was Roy. I looked one last time a few minutes before 8:00AM. It was time to start. We all rose as the judge walked in. I looked again and the court doors were shut. I thought, "I guess he's a no show." It saddened me that he didn't show up. It was hard to explain. I just thought that a father, any father, shouldn't walk away from his child that easily.

I kept looking at the time on my cell phone. It was 10:40AM when they called our name. They cleared the courtroom. Only us, the judge, our lawyers, and the deputies were in the room.

Things began with the judge asking where Roy was. We told him we didn't know. Then the judge asked Donald why he wanted to adopt my daughter. He told the judge he wanted to give her love and stability and a good home. These were all the things she needed. He wanted to be her father in every way.

When the judge read the two letters from Roy, he laughed.

He asked me, "What do you want to do about the past child support that Roy owes?"

I told the judge, "He owes it to her, and I feel he should pay it all."

The judge said, "Ok. It will be reduced, but he will owe it until he pays it in full." Then the adoption was granted. He said, "From this day on your name will be changed to Victoria Reeves and Donald is now your father." I felt so much happiness in the moment. It washed away the sadness, too. I guess in the long run, Roy did what was best for her anyway. Now if she wants him to visit, she can have the say so, but I don't think she will want him to visit.

The adoption was finished. A chapter had closed. My daughter and my husband and I were a family now. No one could say otherwise. He was and still is a father to our daughter. We decided to have her keep using the old name till the school year was finished because we had to get a new birth certificate and new social security card with her new last name.

The next school year, the school wanted me to restore her old last name, because we didn't have the revised birth certificate with her correct name on it. We hadn't gotten it back. We had the original court papers that the judge had signed and stamped. Things went really well after we got things straightened out with her school. Victoria is so happy that her name is changed. She feels a part of Donald's life now. We haven't heard a word from Roy. Every two weeks he sends $39.08. Only time will tell if he will pay the rest of the child support after she turns 18. I doubt that he will. It doesn't matter anyway.

Update as of 2013, December. Roy is still paying back arrearages of child support. He owed $6,000. He was supposed to pay in full by December 16, 2013. I had gotten a letter from the state that they are going after him for the rest of past owed child support. It was not me going after him for the bill. It was the state. The day my husband Donald adopted my daughter April 25, 2009, I didn't care about the owed money, even though I thought Roy should pay.

As for me, I still have panic attacks. I don't know if they will ever end. I do know today I am stronger and a changed woman. I pray my book will inspire you if you are in abusive relationship.

Karla Reeves

- TWENTY-FIVE -

Clarity and Wisdom

I've shared my life with you and by doing so, I have examined my life. I wrote this book to show the different facets of abuse.

I hope that everyone who reads this book learns something new. I hope that people can imagine how someone with a learning disability like myself may find it more difficult to escape. Abusive situations are compounded when you can't read well and don't have a job, a car, or a driver's license.

It may be hard to believe, but some families still raise their daughters to accept that we females are "less than" because we are women. The teaching is very subtle. It may be expressed as a part of the family's faith or just their own up-bringing.

Male headship is supposed to be a biblical tenant, not an excuse to abuse your wife, or to treat them as beneath you. We must find the wisdom that I believe is already planted deep inside of us.

I want people to also see that as abused women, we are broken in spirit. We must stand together as women and men. We must learn how stop the abuse from passing from one generation to the next. We must understand that abuse is often a cycle that perpetuates from generation to generation. It starts with parents who teach and pass on the abuse and pain.

We must wake up and ask, "Why do we live the lives of our parents?" Look at your life. Are you living in the shadow of your mother's life?

We must open our eyes wide and see what is in our own backyard. We must learn to recognize when friends, family, neighbors, or even strangers need help. We must stop this attitude of denial and secrecy.

We should say, "There I go, but by the grace of God." Where is our compassion?

We must get involved and speak up and speak out. When you suspect abuse in your daughter's life, go to her and talk to her. Help her get out. Persist even if she fights with you and defends her abuser.

At least you will know you tried to break that chain. There are clues to abuse. You must be aware and watch how your daughter or son speaks to their partner. Have they changed since they entered into a new relationship? Don't forget, men get abused, too.

I wrote this chapter to remind you that gender, race, and economic status does not preclude abuse. Abuse does not discriminate.

In my circumstances, being young and living in a dysfunctional family made me vulnerable. Economics and an inability to read well or drive a vehicle complicated my ability to escape. But imagine, wealthy people are also in abusive relationships. I am sure that their situation comes with just as many feelings of shame and embarrassment, and has different complications than mine.

Just because you don't see the bruises or broken bones does not mean that abuse is not going on. Just because you can't admit you are in abuse does not mean you're not being abused.

I pray that you examine your life. Did you choose the "bad boy?" Why? Could the roots go as far back as your childhood? Were you being touched by mom's new boyfriend or husband? Why is it okay for you to be hit or yelled at?

We must have compassion for each other, we must reach out to the youth. The young women and men are our tomorrow. We must help them and heal this toxic environment.

We must start with ourselves. We must, as women, teach our young women to be able to depend on themselves. Victims need to reach out to someone and keep talking about abuse until something changes.

It takes so much courage to speak out about abuse. Even writing this book, I know I will make my family members mad. Some of my family don't want me to "air our family's dirty laundry."

I stand in faith and I stand for the truth. Have you ever heard women talking about a family member and speculate, "Wonder what she did to make him hit her?" We must change the way we think. We must not blame the victim.

It is the same with children being sexually abused. I remember when a girl in our neighborhood, who was 14 years old, got pregnant. People who knew her were saying "What a tramp she was for having sex."

My question is, "Where did she learn about having sex at such a young age?" Why do we, as people, turn on the 14-year-old child and kick her when she's down? It turns out that this little 14-year-old girl was raped by her grandfather.

Why did the women in my family keep all that quiet? Rape is a crime. This kind of thing happens in too many families. My family is no different.

The girl tried to tell her mom what happened, and she was accused of lying. Why do we do this? Why is denial our automatic response? We must blame the one who is to blame, not the victim. You may think I am getting off the subject of abuse with all of this blaming and shaming.

I am just asking, "Where do the roots of abuse really come from in your family?" Hitting is not love. A father hits his wife; his son beats his wife. A twisted version of 'love' is being taught, and down the generations it goes, unless we stop it.

We must be mindful every day. What do we teach without saying? Our actions teach deeper lessons than words do. We must try to heal the next generation. I don't know if things will ever be perfect, but we must try for a better tomorrow.

It changes a child's life structure when we stay in abusive relationships. We instill so many messages in our children. I know it's hard to come out of the fog of denial, but we must survive to teach better life lessons.

After I got out of the abusive relationship I had to get into counseling, and I had to re-teach myself what was good love and what was bad love. It is a lesson I will probably keep teaching myself to unlearn the bad habits of having abuse in my life. It was like pulling the layers of my skin off. I had to get counseling to change the way I thought about relationships. Today we can start anew. I pray that this book will touch your heart and soul and help you to heal.

- TWENTY-SIX -

Reflections

I have written this book over a long period of time. Sometimes, God has to place that big life mirror right in front of you. That's what happened to me when I began to see my life through my daughter's relationship.

For four years, my daughter was dating a young man that reminded me of a young Roy. Through her, I could see my life as it was when I was younger. It was scary for me.

I saw my life being repeated through my daughter's relationship. The abuse was moving down the generational line, repeating in my daughter's life. I had unknowingly taught her this pattern. My actions of staying with her birth father had done damage. She had learned it was okay to stay with a controller and an abuser.

The mental abuse that she couldn't see in her relationship was like what I couldn't see in mine all those years earlier.

God was revealing things through my daughter's life and relationships to show me that I had not fully broken the chain of abuse. It had passed down to my daughter. I had to help her see what my husband and I were seeing. It just made me cry. I couldn't stand to see her go down that path.

When I would turn on the Dr. Phil television show, if he had a show on abusive relationships, I would tape the show. When Victoria was home from college, we would watch the show and

211

I would talk to her about abuse. I was using the television show to bring up things that I had gone through with her birth father, hings that she may have buried, or not really understood at the time.

Some people would tell me that I would not be able to reach her about abuse. I would tell them, "You don't know my faith in my God." I knew God would help me say something to reach her. I couldn't give up on my only daughter. I had to reach her somehow.

Things were going on in her relationship that I recognized from my own experience. I was seeing him putting space between her and us. The young man had a temper and that sent up many more red flags.

I didn't give up on her like my best friend didn't give up on me and, most of all, like God didn't give up on me.

Things finally came to a head and she broke things off with him. God has shown me many things. He showed me 20 years of mental and emotional abuse and the total damage it has done to me. God has shown me the damage of my daughter's relationship of four years. I know the damage is reversible. I was healed; she can be healed. And you can be healed.

Victoria now has a true father in her life. He is my new husband, Donald. Donald and I have been married for 11 years. God has truly given me gifts and blessings in my life. Victoria has grown into a beautiful young lady and is now in a relationship with a kind and loving young man. She is attending college in Kentucky and wants to become a teacher. She is now a strong young lady, full of happiness with the love of good parents. She is well-rounded in life.

I am so proud of our daughter. I am praying for God to watch over her and help her through her own life's path.

I hope that I have broken the chain of abuse. I don't want to pass that on to this amazing young woman. My prayer for her is that the things we went through won't leave scars on her heart and bruises on the inside. She is our tomorrow.

*****

Victoria

Postscript

I hope this book can help you see the reasons why you should leave your abusive relationship. I hope this book will give others the knowledge and courage to offer kindness and help to those who are victims of abuse.

I am working on going to women's shelters and churches to speak about abuse. One of my other goals is to speak to young women at colleges about abuse. If my book has inspired you, I would love to hear your personal story. If you know of someone in abuse, or you suspect they are in abuse, reach out to them. Maybe you can help them get out.

I know I don't have all the answers of how to get out of abuse. All relationships are different. Maybe my story can help someone out there who is reading about it here. I hope my book will also help someone understand the mindset of an abused person.

If you are in an abusive relationship, may God bless you and help you to leave safely. If you know of someone who is being abused, may God give you courage to provide the help and encouragement they need.

I would like to hear from you if my book has helped you in your life or just inspired you to get out. We all can help the abused. Sometimes it is just a matter of giving them compassion. Don't turn your back on the victim because they stay with the abuser. The situation is usually more difficult from their perspective than you might think. Sometimes all you can do is give emotional support and pray for them. One day, they may need your help getting out. Never give up on them. Pray for them. They need love, prayers, and your support.

Thank you for buying my book.

My email is kjreeves225@gmail.com or kreeves225@aol.com. For the subject line write BRUISES FROM WITHIN. I am on Facebook, https://www.facebook.com/karla.reeves.52.

*****

God Walked My Path with Me
By Karla Reeves

God took me by the hand. He
walked my path with me
showing me
my journey would not be easy.

He showed me the jagged stairs
made of stone that I would have to walk
in my life's journey.

It began to storm
as I took my first step in life's journey.
The room was dark as I walked to the first step.
I felt the hand of God.

He said, "I am here with you
in the darkness. I will always be here
to hold your hand. My beloved,
I have counted your every tear.
I've placed your tears and prayers
in a heart-shaped bottle. I hold your tears
next to my heart. I give you grace
to walk your life's journey. I will be there
in your darkest times and storms.
I am there with you, my beloved."

I placed my bare foot
on the first jagged stone stairs.
The stone cuts my foot. I stumbled
in the dark stairway and fell.
I felt God's hands holding mine.

I kept walking up the jagged stairs.
My feet hurt so bad from the pain
I walked through. I became weary
as I tried to walk up the stairs.
I fell. I couldn't walk another step.
My feet were bleeding from the cuts.

God picked me up, carried me
up the stone staircase. The light grew
as He put His foot on each jagged step.
I felt the warmth of His healing love
touch my bruises from within.

He let me see my heart as he saw it:

all the bruises from within.
He restored my heart and healed it.
As I looked into God's eyes,
He let me see myself as He saw me.

I felt love like I could ever explain. His love
lifted me up higher than I had ever been.
He has shown me compassion that
I could never have shown myself.
He has shown me forgiveness that
I could never show myself.

My feet and body were healed
from all the pain of 20 years of abuse.
We were nearing the top of the stairs. He put me down.

"You must walk this journey.
I've shown you the way. Know
that I am always here with you.
I am in the darkness. I am in the light.
I am in your heart. I will give you strength
to endure all. Know that I am with you always.

"I walk your journey with you.
Sometimes in the mud you will see
only one set of footprints. They are mine.
I will carry you when you need me.
I am here. You are never alone.
My beloved, I love you."

*****

**If you need help to leave an abusive relationship,
or know someone who does, please call
1-800-799-SAFE(7233). Or call 911 for help.**

Domestic violence statistics

- A person is abused in the United States every 9 seconds. On average, 3 women are killed by a current or former intimate partner each day in the United States. *(Bureau of Justice, Statistics)*
- 1 in 4 women have experienced severe physical violence by an intimate partner. *(National Intimate Partner & Sexual Violence Survey)*
- 66 percent of female stalking victims are stalked by a current or former intimate partner. *(National Stalking Resource Center)*
- Domestic violence costs more than $8.3 billion a year in medical care, mental health services and lost productivity at companies. *(Centers for Disease Control and Prevention)*
- More than 15 million children witness domestic violence each year in the United States. *(Journal of Family Psychology)*
- 1 in 4 women and 1 out of 6 men are sexually abused in their lifetime. *(Department of Justice)*
- In 8 out of 10 rape cases, the victim knows the attacker. *(Department of Justice)*
- 1 in 2 transgender individuals will experience sexual violence. *(National Intimate Partner & Sexual Violence Survey)*
- 1 in 4 bisexual women will experience sexual violence; *(National Intimate Partner & Sexual Violence Survey)*
- 2 in 5 gay men will be sexually abused. *(National Intimate Partner & Sexual Violence Survey)*
- Nearly 6 out of 10 sexual assaults occur in the victim's home or the home of a friend, relative or neighbor. *(Department of Justice)*
- 13.3 percent of college women say they have been forced to have sex in a dating situation. *(Journal of Interpersonal Violence)*

- Only 28 percent of victims report their sexual assault to the police. *(Bureau of Justice Statistics)*
- Only about 2 percent of all sexual assaults reported to police turn out to be false. *(Department of Justice)*
- Among developmentally disabled adults, up to 83 percent of females and 32 percent of males are victims of sexual violence. *(Disabled Women's Network)*

Child abuse statistics

- A report of child abuse is made every 10 seconds. *(American Society for the Positive Care of Children)*
- 1 in 3 girls and 1 in 7 boys will be sexually assaulted by the time they reach 18. *(Department of Justice)*
- More than 4 children die each day because of child abuse. *(U.S. Department of Health and Human Services)*
- More than 90 percent of child sexual abuse victims know their attacker. *("Sexual Assault of Young Children as Reported to Law Enforcement" by Howard Snyder)*
- Approximately 70 percent of children that die from abuse are under the age of 4. *(U.S. Department of Health and Human Services)*
- About 30 percent of abused and neglected children will later abuse their own children, continuing the cycle of violence. *(U.S. Department of Health and Human Services)*

If you need help to leave an abusive relationship, or know someone who does, please call the National Domestic Abuse Hotline: 1-800-799-SAFE(7233). Or call 911 for help.

Karla Reeves

www.ingramcontent.com/pod-product-compliance
Lightning Source LLC
LaVergne TN
LVHW041214080426
835508LV00011B/959